Velma Tours

ST. KITTS AND NEVIS TRAVEL GUIDE 2023

Pocket Guide to Unveils the Treasures of the Twin Islands, Discover Its Hidden Gems, Culture, History, Food, and Sightseeing Places with a 10-Day Itinerary

Table of Contents

Introduction

My Beautiful Experience in St. Kitts and Nevis

I first saw the stunning St. Kitts and Nevis islands, which are in the middle of the Caribbean Sea, as the plane descended. I could already tell that this vacation would be magical. The warm breeze carried a sense of adventure and relaxation that would make me stay one to remember from the moment I stepped onto the shores.

Upon landing at the Robert L. Bradshaw Worldwide Air terminal in St. Kitts, I was welcomed by cordial local people with comforting grins and an enthusiastic calypso band. It in a flash set the vibe for my excursion in this energetic and socially rich objective. In Basseterre, the capital, I stayed in a charming guesthouse before going to Independence Square and the National Museum, two of the country's historical attractions. I indulged in the tantalizing flavors of Caribbean cuisine at a local restaurant as the sun went down.

I chose to leave on a road trip to the Brimstone Slope Fort Public Park, a UNESCO World Legacy Site. The fortifications' breathtaking panoramic views were simply breathtaking. I couldn't help but take a lot of pictures of the island's green waters and lush landscapes. With the help of knowledgeable guides, the fortress's rich history came to life, transporting me back to a time when it was a stronghold against invading powers.

The pristine beaches on St. Kitts and Nevis are an essential part of any trip. I made my way to the famous Pinney's Beach in Nevis, where the Caribbean Sea's gentle waves met the sparkling white sand. I savored the quiet climate, relaxing under the influencing palm trees and taking reviving plunges in the clear waters. The day was a blissful escape from the daily grind.

I decided to go on a guided hike through the lush rainforests of St. Kitts because I wanted to see the natural beauty of the islands. I was astonished by the tropical fauna and flora as I walked along well-marked trails amid the sounds of chirping birds and rustling leaves. Reaching the summit of Mount Liamuiga, the dormant volcano that dominates the island's landscape, was my reward for my efforts. Remaining at the highest point, I felt a staggering feeling of achievement and a significant association with nature.

To dive further into the islands' set of experiences, I visited the captivating memorable manors that have been safeguarded throughout the long term. The flawlessly reestablished Romney Estate, when a sugarcane ranch, presently houses an enrapturing greenhouse loaded up with lively tropical blossoms and a great saman tree. I was able to reflect on the island's intricate history after exploring these plantations, which provided a window into the past.

The culinary pleasures of St. Kitts and Nevis were a disclosure. I savored the flavorful meals that were made with ingredients that were sourced locally and ate seafood that was just caught. One of the features was a visit to an enthusiastic neighborhood market, where I communicated with well-disposed merchants, examined outlandish natural products and enjoyed customary dishes like goat water stew and conch squanders. It was a vivid encounter that added a layer of validness to my excursion.

As the last day of my excursion drew nearer, I wanted to feel a hint of pity. My time in St. Kitts and Nevis had been full of amazing experiences, beautiful scenery that will stay with me forever, and genuine hospitality. I said my goodbyes to the islands knowing that I would always treasure the experiences of this journey.

My visit to St. Kitts and Nevis surpassed all assumptions, making a permanent imprint on my spirit. I was blown away by the islands' immersive experience, which included everything from the stunning natural wonders and rich cultural heritage to the friendly locals. I knew as soon as I got on the plane to go back home that this amazing journey was just the beginning of a love affair with this Caribbean paradise that would last a lifetime.

Welcome to St. Kitts and Nevis

St. Kitts and Nevis are genuinely heaven in the Caribbean, offering a variety of normal marvels, rich history, and social encounters. Whether you look for unwinding on flawless sea shores, set out on exciting open-air experiences, or drench yourself in the islands' energetic culture, St. Kitts and Nevis bring something to the table for each voyager. Find this charming objective, where stunning scenes and warm friendliness join to make recollections that will endure forever.

These two islands combine breathtaking natural beauty, a long history, a vibrant culture, and warm hospitality in a novel way. From flawless sea shores to rich rainforests and authentic milestones, St. Kitts and Nevis enrapture guests with their enthralling appeal. Take a comprehensive journey with us as we discover the wonders of this Caribbean haven.

Geography and Climate

St. Kitts and Nevis are located in the eastern Caribbean, just west of Antigua and Barbuda. St. Kitts, the larger of the two islands, boasts volcanic peaks, including Mount

Liamuiga, while Nevis is known for its rolling hills and scenic landscapes. The islands are blessed with a tropical climate, characterized by year-round warm temperatures, making it an ideal destination for sun-seekers and nature enthusiasts alike. The dry season, from December to April, offers the most favorable weather for outdoor activities, while the rainy season, from May to November, showcases the islands' lush greenery.

History and Cultural Heritage

St. Kitts and Nevis, which is steeped in history and has witnessed the rise and fall of empires, is a treasure trove of cultural heritage. Before Christopher Columbus arrived in 1493, indigenous peoples lived on the islands. They later turned into a milestone for European powers competing for control, bringing about an interesting mix of European, African, and Caribbean impacts.

The Brimstone Hill Fortress National Park in St. Kitts is one of the most significant historical sites. With its impressive fortifications and breathtaking views, this UNESCO World Heritage Site provides a glimpse into the island's colonial past. The capital city of Basseterre is additionally saturated with history, including frontier-time engineering, for example, Freedom Square and the Georgian-style Government House.

The way of life of St. Kitts and Nevis is dynamic and various, with a profound appreciation for music, dance, and narrating. Calypso and reggae's pulsating beats can be heard all over the islands, especially at the St. Kitts Music Festival, where well-known local and international artists perform. The Fair festivals, held in December and January, are lively scenes of vivid ensembles, vigorous processions, and throbbing music.

Natural Wonders and Outdoor Adventures

With its numerous natural wonders and thrilling activities, St. Kitts and Nevis is a playground for outdoor enthusiasts. The islands are famous for their unblemished sea shores, with fine white sands and turquoise waters. Pinney's Beach in Nevis and Frigate Bay in St. Kitts are two popular beaches where tourists can relax in the sun, swim in crystal-clear waters, or try new water sports like snorkeling, scuba diving, and kayaking.

The St. Kitts rainforests offer numerous opportunities for hiking, nature walks, and zip lining for adrenaline junkies. The climb to Mount Liamuiga's summit is a challenging but rewarding adventure that gives you a view of the surrounding islands and the chance to explore the volcano's crater. In the lush rainforest reserves, nature lovers can also find rare plants and animals like vervet monkeys and tropical bird species.

Historical Landmarks and Cultural Experiences

Delve into the island's captivating history by exploring the numerous historical landmarks and cultural sites. Romney Manor, a former sugarcane plantation, is now home to the Caribelle Batik workshop, where visitors can witness the intricate art of batik-making and purchase beautifully crafted textiles. The Alexander Hamilton House in Charlestown, Nevis, is another must-visit attraction, providing insights into the early life of the founding father of the United States.

To immerse yourself in the vibrant local culture, visit the island's many festivals and events. The annual St. Kitts-Nevis National Carnival, known as Sugar Mas, is a grand celebration of music, dance, and vibrant costumes. The Green Valley Festival in Nevis showcases traditional folk dances and music, while the St. Kitts Music Festival attracts internationally renowned artists and offers a unique fusion of musical genres.

Culinary Delights and Local Cuisine

Indulging in the delectable cuisine of St. Kitts and Nevis is an essential part of any trip to the island nation. African, European, and Indian flavors have influenced the islands' culinary traditions. The local dishes feature a lot of fresh seafood, like lobster, snapper, conch, and other types of fish. "Stewed Saltfish and Johnny Cake," the country's national dish, is a savory delight made with fried dough and salted codfish. Other well-known dishes incorporate "Goat Water," a generous stew, and "Pelau," a one-pot rice dish with chicken or hamburger.

Visit local eateries, beachside shacks, and fine-dining restaurants to taste the island's vibrant flavors. While taking in the stunning sunsets of the Caribbean, don't miss out on the opportunity to sip on a locally brewed "Carib" beer or a refreshing "Brimstone Rum Punch."

Hospitality and Accommodation

A trip to the islands is enhanced by the welcoming spirit of the Kittitian and Nevisian people. From comfortable guesthouses and shop inns to extravagance resorts, St. Kitts and Nevis offer a scope of facilities to suit each voyager's requirements. Spas, golf courses, and swimming pools are just some of the world-class amenities offered by many resorts, which also provide direct access to the beaches.

My Top 15 Reasons for Visiting St. Kitts and Nevis

Travelers from all over the world are drawn to St. Kitts and Nevis because of its captivating combination of natural beauty, rich history, vibrant culture, and warm hospitality. From the immaculate sea shores and submerged marvels to the verifiable milestones and social merriments, these islands bring something to the table for each guest. Each beach has its distinct charm and breathtaking beauty, from the well-known Pinney's Beach in Nevis to the lively Frigate Bay in St. Kitts people's

Diving and Snorkeling

Under the shimmering waters encompassing St. Kitts and Nevis lies an entrancing submerged world ready to be investigated. Divers can choose from a wide range of dive spots on the islands, including shipwrecks, underwater caves, and vibrant coral reefs. Swimmers and scuba jumpers can experience a wealth of marine life, from vivid exotic fish to magnificent ocean turtles and, surprisingly, a periodic dolphin or whale.

Hiking and Nature Trails

St. Kitts and Nevis have a plethora of hiking and nature trails for nature lovers that will take you through lush rainforests, up towering mountains, and to hidden waterfalls. A must-do activity is a hike up Mount Liamuiga, a dormant volcano. The breathtaking panoramic view of the entire island is the reward at the summit. There are likewise directed climbs accessible, permitting you to find out about the islands' assorted greenery from proficient nearby aides.

Historic Landmarks

The islands' rich history is obvious in the various noteworthy milestones and destinations that speck the scene. The UNESCO World Heritage-listed Brimstone Hill Fortress National Park is one such landmark. Views of the surrounding countryside and a glimpse into the island's colonial past can be enjoyed from this magnificent fortress. Other eminent destinations incorporate the Romney Estate, where a sugarcane manor and presently home to a lovely greenhouse, and the Alexander Hamilton House, the origination of one of the US's principal architects.

Vibrant Culture and Festivals

The vibrant culture of St. Kitts and Nevis is influenced by African, European, and Caribbean customs. During their annual festivals and events, the islands come to life. The St. Kitts Live performance draws in famous neighborhood and global craftsmen, offering a combination of melodic classifications. Sugar Mas, or the celebrations of Carnival, feature vibrant costumes, vibrant parades, and pulsating music. The opportunity to immerse oneself in the islands' infectious energy and rich cultural heritage is provided by these celebrations.

Delicious Cuisine

Food fans will get a kick out of the kinds of Kittitian and Nevisian cooking. The islands offer different luscious dishes impacted by African, European, and Indian flavors. The local cuisine entices the palate with hearty stews like "Goat Water" and flavorful rice dishes like "Pelau," as well as fresh seafood like lobster and conch. The island's most popular drink, the "Brimstone Rum Punch," is a must-try, as is the island's refreshing "Carib" beer.

Exquisite Wildlife

On land and in the sea, St. Kitts and Nevis are home to a wide variety of wildlife. Nature sweethearts will have the chance to recognize vervet monkeys swinging through the treetops, lively bird species, and marine animals like ocean turtles and dolphins. The islands' dedication to conservation ensures the preservation of these valuable habitats, allowing visitors to appreciate nature's wonders in person.

Luxury Resorts and Accommodations

The islands of St. Kitts and Nevis have a wide selection of opulent resorts and lodging options for discerning travelers. From oceanfront retreats with private manors and limitless pools to store lodgings settled amid lavish nurseries, these facilities give top-notch conveniences and unrivaled solace. Enjoy stunning views of the Caribbean Sea and the islands' natural splendor while submerging yourself in luxury.

Authentic Caribbean Hospitality

The glow and benevolence of the Kittitian and Nevisian individuals are unbelievable. Visitors are made to feel like they are a part of the community by being greeted with genuine smiles and a warm welcome. Local people are dependably anxious to share their insights, stories, and proposals, guaranteeing that your experience on the islands is remarkable.

Island-Hopping and Exploring Nevis

As twin islands, St. Kitts and Nevis offer the chance for extraordinary island-jumping experiences. A short boat ride from St. Kitts takes you to the peaceful island of Nevis, known for its tranquil appeal and untainted regular magnificence. Investigate the memorable capital of Charlestown, visit the origination of Alexander Hamilton, or loosen up on the unspoiled sea shores encompassed by lavish vegetation.

Golfing Paradise

St. Kitts and Nevis has some of the best golfing in the Caribbean, set in beautiful scenery. The Illustrious St. Kitts Golf Club flaunts a title 18-opening course that breezes through lavish vegetation and offers all-encompassing perspectives on the Caribbean Ocean. The difficult fairways and very much manicured greens give the ideal setting for a significant round of golf.

Catamaran Cruises and Sailing Adventures

Take a catamaran cruise or a sailing adventure to fully appreciate the Caribbean Sea's beauty. Loosen up at hand as you sail along the shore, swim in confined bays, or essentially absorb the sun while appreciating reviving refreshments and flavorful neighborhood snacks. These cruises give you a unique look at the islands and the chance to see marine life in its natural environment.

Eco-Tourism and Sustainability

St. Kitts and Nevis is committed to eco-friendly practices and sustainable tourism. To preserve the islands' natural beauty, numerous tour operators and lodgings adhere to stringent environmental regulations. Eco-the-travel industry drives incorporate nature strolls, birdwatching visits, and instructive projects that bring issues to light about the significance of preservation. By visiting these islands, you add to the conservation of their extraordinary biological systems.

Shopping for Local Crafts and Souvenirs

In St. Kitts and Nevis, going to the local markets and craft shops is a wonderful experience. A bustling market in Basseterre, the vibrant capital, is where you can find locally made crafts, spices, artwork, souvenirs, and more. In Romney Manor, the Caribelle Batik workshop lets you see how to make traditional batiks and buy one-of-a-kind textiles. You can bring back a piece of the culture and craftsmanship of the islands with these authentic keepsakes.

Unforgettable Sunsets and Natural Beauty

Some of the Caribbean's most stunning sunsets can be found on St. Kitts and Nevis. The sky changes into a mesmerizing palette of vivid colors as the sun dips below the horizon, creating a magical glow over the islands. These sunsets create unforgettable memories whether you're strolling along the beach, sailing in the Caribbean, or having a romantic dinner at a waterfront restaurant.

10 Interesting Facts No One Tells You About St. Kitts and Nevis

St. Kitts and Nevis, the captivating twin islands settled in the Caribbean Ocean, are prestigious for their perfect sea shores, rich scenes, and warm cordiality. Even though these islands are popular with tourists, some interesting facts are often overlooked. In this chapter, I will provide you with a better understanding and appreciation of St. Kitts and Nevis by revealing ten fascinating facts about the islands.

1. Birthplace of Alexander Hamilton

The fact that Alexander Hamilton, one of the United States Founding Fathers and the first Secretary of the Treasury, was born on the island of Nevis is a fascinating fact about St. Kitts and Nevis. The Alexander Hamilton House is a historic location where visitors can learn about Hamilton's early life and the impact he had on American history.

2. UNESCO World Heritage Site - Brimstone Hill Fortress

St. Kitts is home to the noteworthy Brimstone Slope Fortification, which has been assigned as a UNESCO World Legacy Site. This noteworthy fort is a demonstration of the islands' frontier past and offers all-encompassing perspectives on the encompassing open country and adjoining islands. It grandstands the compositional and designing ability of the English military during the seventeenth and eighteenth hundreds years.

3. Sugar Cane History and the Sugar Train

St. Kitts and Nevis have a long history of sugar stick creation, which assumed a huge part in the islands' economy. Even though sugar production has decreased, the industry is still present. The St. Kitts Grand Railroad, otherwise called the Sugar Train, takes guests on a nostalgic excursion through the island's beautiful open country, passing by previous sugar bequests and giving looks into the islands' sugar stick legacy.

4. Caribelle Batik - A Unique Art Form

At Caribelle Batik, the art of batik making has a home on St. Kitts. Situated in Romney Estate, this studio grandstands the perplexing system of making batik materials. Guests can observe talented craftsman applying wax and dynamic colors to texture, bringing about interesting and vivid plans. Products made of batik, such as clothing, accessories, and home decor, are available in a wide variety at the Caribelle Batik shop.

5. The Railway That Circles Nevis

While St. Kitts has the Sugar Train, Nevis flaunts its novel rail line framework. The Nevisian Legacy Town Rail line takes travelers on a grand excursion through the island's open country, passing verifiable milestones, ranches, and beautiful scenes. The island's fascinating past and stunning natural beauty can be enjoyed delightfully on this narrow-gauge train.

6. Vervet Monkeys - A Quirky Population

Vervet monkeys are a quirky and naughty species that live in St. Kitts. These jovial creatures, which arrived on the island centuries ago, have adapted to and thrived in their lush surroundings. They are often seen swinging through the trees or having fun close to popular tourist attractions.

However, because they are wild animals, it is essential to observe them from a distance and not feed them.

7. The Original Name of St. Kitts

St. Kitts has gone through a few name changes over now is the ideal time. The island's abundant volcanic soil was referred to as "fertile land" by the indigenous people as "Liamuiga." At the point when Christopher Columbus showed up in 1493, he named the island "St. Christopher" after his benefactor holy person. The name was eventually changed to "St. Kitts," which is still used a lot today.

8. The Dual Island Nation

St. Kitts and Nevis are alluded to as a "double island country" because of their one-of-a-kind political design. The Federation of St. Kitts and Nevis unites the two islands, despite their independence. Although each island has its local government, they share a central government and are internationally recognized as a single nation.

9. The Green Vervet Monkey as a National Symbol

The vervet monkey is regarded as a national symbol and holds a special place in the hearts of the Kittitian and Nevisian people. It symbolizes the biodiversity of the islands as well as the peaceful coexistence of humans and nature. The green vervet monkey is highlighted on the crest, money, and different trinkets, filling in as a sign of the islands' novel untamed life.

10. The Smallest Nation in the Western Hemisphere

In terms of both land area and population, St. Kitts and Nevis is the smallest country in the Western Hemisphere. With an all-out land area of only 104 square miles (269 square kilometers) and a populace of around 55,000 individuals, these islands offer a feeling of closeness and quietness that is frequently pursued by voyagers searching for a genuine and uncrowded Caribbean experience.

Getting into the Island

Understanding the History and the Culture

Visitors to St. Kitts and Nevis can gain a deeper appreciation for the islands' heritage and gain insight into the lives of the people who live there by learning about their history and culture.

The historical backdrop of St. Kitts and Nevis traces back to the pre-Columbian time when the islands were occupied by the native Kalinago individuals. The appearance of European voyagers in the late fifteenth hundred years, including Christopher Columbus, denoted the start of another part of the islands' set of experiences. The British and French, along with other European powers, fought for control of the islands, resulting in a turbulent colonization and dominance struggle.

The development of the sugar industry in the 17th and 18th centuries is one significant event in the history of St. Kitts and Nevis. The islands became significant makers of sugar, and their economies were based on the work of oppressed Africans who were effectively brought to chip away at the estates. The remainders of the sugar business, for example, old manor domains and sugar plants, can, in any case, be tracked down on the islands today, filling in as tokens of this dull part ever.

The battle for the opportunity and the nullification of servitude likewise assumed a critical part in molding the islands' set of experiences. In 1834, the British colonies of St. Kitts and Nevis became the first in the Caribbean to abolish slavery. The fight for emancipation and the legacy of slavery are deeply ingrained in the culture of the islands. Various commemorative events and monuments, such as Emancipation Day celebrations and the National Heroes Park, which honors the nation's freedom fighters, serve as reminders of these events.

The diverse influences of the indigenous, African, European, and East Indian populations of St. Kitts and Nevis create a rich cultural tapestry. Festivals, music, dance, and food from the islands all reflect this fusion of cultures. Calypso and reggae music are famous sorts that grandstand the lively melodic legacy of the islands. Throughout the year, you can hear the pulsating rhythms and lively melodies of these musical styles at local festivals and events.

The cuisine of St. Kitts and Nevis reflects the islands' cultural diversity. Customary dishes, for example, goat water (a good stew), saltfish, and conch wastes are famous staples. The flavors are a tempting mix of African, European, and Creole impacts. During community cookouts known as "lime sessions," where friends and family gather to share food, music, and laughter, visitors can enjoy the island's culinary delights at local restaurants, street food stalls, and other venues.

Workmanship and art likewise hold a huge spot in the social scene of St. Kitts and Nevis. Beautiful pottery, woodcarvings, and baskets made by local artisans demonstrate their creativity and skill. These artistic expressions frequently get their ideas from the natural beauty of the islands and the traditions that have been passed down through the generations.

Religion is a fundamental piece of the way of life in St. Kitts and Nevis, with Christianity being the predominant confidence. Numerous churches dot the islands, some of which are architectural treasures with historical significance. Strict celebrations and functions assume a fundamental part in the existence of the islanders, encouraging a feeling of the local area and otherworldly association.

My Best 15 Things to do in St. Kitts and Nevis

The islands have something for everyone, from historic landmarks to pristine beaches to vibrant culture to lush rainforests. To make sure that every visitor to St. Kitts and Nevis has an unforgettable time, I have compiled a list of the 15 best things to do there.

1. Explore the National Park of Brimstone Hill Fortress

Visit the Brimstone Hill Fortress, a UNESCO World Heritage Site, to begin your journey. This seventeenth-century fort brags all-encompassing perspectives on the Caribbean Ocean and features the islands' frontier past. Investigate the very much-protected strongholds, appreciate the verifiable displays, and absorb the stunning landscape.

2. Mount Liamuiga hike

A hike up Mount Liamuiga is a must-do for adventurers. The 3,792-foot trek to this dormant volcano is both challenging and rewarding. Reach the summit for a jaw-dropping view of the islands that surround you as you meander through lush rainforests and observe one-of-a-kind plants and animals.

3. Find the Appeal of Basseterre

Take a stroll through Basseterre, the capital, and take in the vibrant atmosphere. Visit St. George's Anglican Church, Independence Square, and the local markets and shops for handicrafts and souvenirs. Make sure to try the local street food for a mouthwatering meal.

4. At Cockleshell Beach, unwind

Enjoy the flawless excellence of Cockleshell Ocean side, situated on the southern bank of St. Kitts. This beach is a haven for sunbathing, swimming, and snorkeling thanks to its powdery white sand, clear water, and stunning Nevis views. At the nearby beach bars, you can dine on the beach and sip refreshing cocktails.

5. Take a Cruise on a Catamaran

Take a Catamaran cruise to see the islands and the turquoise waters that surround them. Sail along the shore, swim in lively coral reefs, and partake in a lavish Caribbean-style lunch ready. Some cruises even provide guests with the opportunity to swim with sea turtles, making it a truly memorable experience.

6. Make a trip to Caribelle Batik

At Caribelle Batik, a charming shop in Romney Manor, learn about the art of batik. Watch as traditional methods are used by local artisans to create intricate designs on fabric. Take home some one-of-a-kind batik mementos by exploring the stunning botanical gardens surrounding the shop.

7. At the Museum of Nevis History, immerse yourself in history

Excursion to Nevis and visit the Gallery of Nevis History, situated in Charlestown. Discover the island's fascinating past, including its connection to one of America's Founding

Fathers, Alexander Hamilton. Explore photographs, artifacts, and documents that provide insight into Nevis's varied past.

8. Take a look at the forest

Set out on a rainforest experience and find the rich excellence of St. Kitts' inside. Listen to the sounds of tropical birds as you hike along trails surrounded by towering trees, marvel at stunning waterfalls like the Wingfield River Falls, and more. The rainforest's unique flora and fauna can be better understood on guided tours.

9. Experience Fair

If you can visit during the Carnival season, take part in the lively celebrations. Take pleasure in the lively music, intricate costumes, vibrant parades, and contagious energy of the locals. The Festival is a genuine impression of the islands' rich social legacy and a demonstration of their soul and happiness.

10. In the Shitten Bay Marine Reserve, dive or snorkel

Dig into the submerged universe of St. Kitts and Nevis by investigating the Shitten Narrows Marine Save. Scuba or snorkel in the crystal-clear waters filled with colorful coral reefs, ancient shipwrecks, and marine life. Experienced jumpers and amateurs can track down reasonable spots for investigation.

11. Royal St. Kitts Golf Club

Golf devotees can start at the Imperial St. Kitts Golf Club, which offers amazing perspectives on both the Caribbean Ocean and the Atlantic Sea. This 18-opening title fairway challenges players of all levels while giving an important playing golf insight into the midst of the tropical landscape.

12. Find the Dark Rocks

Witness the strong powers of nature at the Dark Shakes, a characteristic development of volcanic rocks on the northeastern shore of St. Kitts. A striking and attractive scene is created by the stark contrast between the green landscape, crashing waves, and black rocks.

13. Beach Riding on Horseback

Riding a horse along the dunes of St. Kitts or Nevis is a thrilling activity. Riders of all skill levels can take guided tours of the island's scenic coastline to see breathtaking views and get a different perspective on the island's beauty.

14. Enjoy local cuisine

Savoring the cuisine of St. Kitts and Nevis is an essential part of any trip there. Try dishes like "stewed saltfish," "goat water," and "spiced lobster" that will make you hungry. To enjoy the island's authentic flavors and the warmth of Kittitian and Nevisian hospitality, go to beachside shacks and local restaurants.

15. Go to a Live concert

If you're a music sweetheart, plan your visit to match with one of the islands' exuberant live performances. The St. Kitts Music Festival and the Nevis Blues Festival offer an unforgettable experience of captivating performances and infectious rhythms by showcasing local and international talent.

My Best 15 Things NOT to do in St. Kitts and Nevis

St. Kitts and Nevis, the delightful twin-island country situated in the Caribbean, offer an abundance of attractions and exercises for guests to appreciate. In any case, it's likewise vital to know about specific things that ought to be kept away from to guarantee a protected, conscious, and charming experience. I've compiled a list of the 15 things you shouldn't do in St. Kitts and Nevis to make your trip easier.

1. **Try not to Overlook Nearby Traditions and Behavior**: It is essential to familiarize yourself with the etiquette and customs of St. Kitts and Nevis to demonstrate respect for the culture of the country. Keep away from the impolite way of behaving, like wearing swimwear beyond assigned regions, and consistently request authorization before taking photos from local people.

2. **Try not to Insolence the Climate**: St. Kitts and Nevis are known for their immaculate normal excellence.

Abstain from littering, harming coral reefs while swimming or plunging, or upsetting untamed life. Regard the climate by rehearsing mindful of the travel industry and adhering to assigned trails and rules.

3. **Animals shouldn't be fed or disturbed**: Although feeding or disturbing animals can hurt their natural behavior and ecosystem, it is tempting to interact with wildlife. Keep a deferential separation and notice them right at home without meddling.

4. **Do not consume tap water**: In St. Kitts and Nevis, tap water should not be consumed. If you want to keep your health and avoid getting sick, use water purification methods or buy water in bottles.

5. **Keep sun protection in mind**: The Caribbean sun can be serious. Remember to safeguard yourself from sun-related burn by wearing sunscreen, caps, and shades. To avoid becoming dehydrated, seek shade during the hottest parts of the day and drink plenty of water.

6. **Try not to Neglect Wellbeing Safety Measures**: Even though St. Kitts and Nevis are generally safe places to visit, it is still important to take the most fundamental safety measures. Be careful when participating in water sports or other outdoor activities, keep an eye on your belongings, and avoid walking alone at night in areas that are unfamiliar or poorly lit.

7. **Respect Historic Monuments and Sites:** Brimstone Hill Fortress is one of many historical landmarks and sites on the islands. Respect these significant landmarks by adhering to the rules, not damaging or climbing on structures, and not littering in these areas.

8. **Remember to treat private property with respect**: Avoid entering private property without permission and be mindful of private property. Respect the privacy of the residents and abide by any restrictions or signs that are in place.

9. **Try not to Swim in Unprotected Regions**: St. Kitts and Nevis have beautiful beaches, but there may be undertows or strong currents in some places. Always follow the advice of lifeguards and avoid swimming in areas that are not marked or guarded.

10. **Try not to Climb Alone in Distant Regions:** On the off chance that you intend to go climbing, particularly in distant regions, it is prudent to avoid it single-handedly. Always tell someone about your plans, stick to trails that have been marked, and bring water, snacks, and a map with you.

11. **Do not Consume Drugs**: In St. Kitts and Nevis, it is illegal to use drugs, including marijuana. To avoid legal repercussions and potential dangers to your health and safety, don't use illegal substances.

12. **Protect yourself from mosquitoes**: In tropical areas, mosquitoes can be common. Safeguard yourself from mosquito-borne sicknesses by utilizing anti-agents,

wearing long sleeves and jeans, and remaining in facilities with screens or cooling.

13. **Try not to Drive Without a Substantial Permit:** Make sure you have a current driver's license if you want to rent a car. To ensure a hassle-free and safe trip, familiarize yourself with local driving regulations and obey traffic laws.

14. **Don't ignore warnings about the weather**: Hurricanes and tropical storms are possible in the Caribbean. Follow any local authorities' warnings or advisories, as well as the weather forecasts. Prepare as necessary and comply with evacuation instructions if necessary.

15. **Local Experiences Should Not Be Missed:** Last but not least, don't pass up the chance to learn about the local cuisine, customs, and culture. To truly appreciate the islands' singular charm, interact with the welcoming locals, sample authentic Nevisian and Kittitian cuisine, and take part in cultural activities.

Do I need a Visa to Visit the Island?

One of the most important things to think about if you want to visit an island is whether you need a visa to enter. The requirements for obtaining a visa in St. Kitts and Nevis, a Caribbean nation with two islands, may vary based on your nationality as well as the purpose and length of your visit. In this far-reaching chapter, I will provide you with the visa prerequisites for visiting St. Kitts and Nevis, assisting you with understanding whether you want a visa and how to explore the cycle.

Visa-Free Entry:

St. Kitts and Nevis offer visa passage to residents of numerous nations for shifting times of stay. By and large, guests from nations, for example, the US, Canada, the Unified Realm, European Endorser states, Australia, and New Zealand can enter the islands for travel industry purposes without a visa. Depending on the nation of citizenship, the maximum length of stay that is permitted can be anywhere from 30 to 90 days. It is essential to keep in mind that visa-free entry typically only applies to tourism and may not cover employment or business-related activities.

Visa-On-Arrival:

Some nationalities that are not eligible for visa-free entry may have the option of obtaining a visa upon arrival in St. Kitts and Nevis. The visa-on-arrival allows visitors to obtain a visa at the port of entry, such as the Robert L. Bradshaw International Airport or the Vance W. Amory International Airport. The visa-on-arrival is typically issued for a limited duration, usually ranging from 30 to 90 days, depending on the purpose of the visit. It's crucial to check whether your nationality is eligible for visa-on-arrival and the specific requirements and conditions associated with it.

Visa-Required Countries:

Before visiting St. Kitts and Nevis, nationals of certain nations must obtain a visa. If your nation is on the rundown of visa-required nations, you should apply for a visa at the closest St. Kitts and Nevis discretionary mission or office before your outing. A completed application form, a valid passport, proof of accommodation, proof of sufficient funds, and a return ticket are typically required to complete the visa application process. It's prudent to start the visa application process well ahead of time to take into account adequate handling time.

Visa Extensions:

On the off chance that you wish to expand your visit past the allowed term, it very well might be feasible to apply for a visa expansion while in St. Kitts and Nevis. The expansion should be mentioned before the lapse of your underlying visa or sans visa period. The interaction for visa expansions regularly includes presenting an application, giving substantial motivation to the augmentation, and paying the necessary charges. It is essential to keep in mind that the immigration authorities may or may not grant visa extensions at their discretion.

Other Visa Categories:

St. Kitts and Nevis offers additional visa categories for specific purposes, including business, employment, education, and medical treatment, in addition to tourist visas. It is essential to select the appropriate visa category and meet the specific requirements for that category if you intend to visit for purposes other than tourism. Counseling the authority site of the St is prudent. Kitts and Nevis Service of International concerns or contact the closest political mission or department for the most cutting-edge data on visa prerequisites and application methods.

Travel Documents:

Check that your travel documents, particularly your passport, meet the requirements in addition to the requirements for a visa. Your identification ought to be legitimate for somewhere around a half year past your expected flight date from St. Kitts and Nevis. Additionally, there should be enough blank pages for visa stamps on it.

Seek Professional Advice:

Navigating the requirements of a visa can occasionally be difficult, particularly if you have particular circumstances or are unsure of your eligibility. In such instances, it is advised to seek professional guidance from immigration lawyers or visa service providers who are knowledgeable about the requirements for St. Kitts and Nevis visas. They can assist you with the visa application process and provide individualized guidance based on your specific circumstances.

Program for Visa Waiver

An initiative known as the Program for Visa Waiver, also referred to as the Visa Waiver Program (VWP), makes it possible for citizens of certain nations to travel to other nations for business or tourism purposes without requiring a traditional visa. The program plans to advance travel and upgrade financial and social ties between taking part nations.

What is the Program for Visa Waiver?

The Program for Visa Waiver empowers residents of explicit nations to make a trip to taking an interest nation for momentary visits without the requirement for a visa. Eligible travelers can apply for an electronic travel authorization online instead of applying for a visa at an embassy or consulate, which simplifies the process and reduces the amount of paperwork required.

Benefits of the Program:

There are several advantages for both travelers and host nations from the Program for Visa Waiver. It simplifies and makes it easier for travelers to visit other countries without needing a traditional visa. It reduces paperwork, saves time, and eliminates in-person interviews. Additionally, it fosters international cooperation and understanding by promoting tourism, business exchanges, and cultural interactions.

Participating Countries:

There are bilateral agreements between nations involved in the Program for Visa Waiver. Not all nations take part in the program, and qualifications might change relying upon the particular arrangements set up. For instance, the US works the notable Visa Waiver Program (VWP), which permits residents from taking part nations to enter the US for as long as 90 days for the travel industry or business purposes without a visa. There are also visa waiver programs in Australia, Canada, and the member states of the European Union.

Eligibility Criteria:

To be qualified for the Program for Visa Waiver, explorers should meet specific measures. These requirements may include possessing a valid passport from a participating nation, intending to travel solely for tourism or business, possessing a ticket for return or onward travel, and staying for a predetermined amount of time, typically 90 days. Additionally, travelers must not pose a security threat to the host nation and must not have a criminal record or previous visa violations.

Electronic Travel Authorization (ETA):

Electronic travel authorization, or ETA, is what the Program for Visa Waiver requires of travelers. The estimated time of arrival is an electronic record that awards consent to make a trip to the host country. Most of the time, the application process entails filling out a form online, providing personal information, and details about a passport, travel plans, and answering security-related questions. After that, the application is looked over, and the ETA is given out electronically if it is approved.

Validity and Restrictions:

The legitimacy time frame and states of the electronic travel approval can differ contingent upon the taking part nations. Most of the time, the ETA is good for multiple entries within a certain amount of time, like two years. Be that as it may, the length of every individual stay is by and large restricted to 90 days. As overstaying a permit can have serious repercussions, it is critical to adhere to the stipulated conditions, including leaving before the authorized period.

Extension and Conversion:

The Program for Visa Waiver typically prevents the waiver from being extended or converted to a different visa category. If a voyager wishes to remain longer, work, study, or participate in exercises not allowed under the visa waiver, they would have to leave the country before the approved period closes and apply for the fitting visa through the normal channels.

Preparing for Travel:

Before going under the Program for Visa Waiver, it's vital to satisfactorily plan. This includes making sure the passport is still valid at least six months after the intended departure date, learning about the specific requirements and terms of the host country's visa waiver program, and showing that you have enough money to cover the costs of the trip.

Compliance and Legal Considerations:

Even though the Program Visa Waiver makes getting in easier, you still need to follow the rules and laws of the country where you're staying. Visitors must adhere to local laws and regulations, observe the terms of their authorized stay, and refrain from engaging in prohibited activities like unauthorized employment.

Future Changes and Updates:

The eligibility criteria, conditions, and procedures for the Program for Visa Waiver may be reviewed and updated regularly by the participating nations. It's vital to remain informed about any progressions to guarantee consistence and avoid any issues during movement.

The Best Way to Move into St. Kitts and Nevis? (By Air, Sea)

Whether you're arranging an excursion or taking into account a more long-lasting move to the islands, it's fundamental to comprehend the most effective ways to make a trip to St. Kitts and Nevis. In this section, I will guide you through the transportation choices accessible, including air travel and sea travel, assisting you with settling on an educated conclusion about the most effective way to move into St. Kitts and Nevis.

Air Travel:

The most common and convenient way to get to St. Kitts and Nevis is by plane. There are two international airports serving the islands: Vance W. Amory International Airport (NEV) is on Nevis, and Robert L. Bradshaw International Airport (SKB) is on St. Kitts. This is the very thing you want to realize about air travel to St. Kitts and Nevis:

a. International Flights:

Several international airlines operate regular flights to St. Kitts and Nevis, connecting the islands with major cities in North America, Europe, and the Caribbean. Airlines such as American Airlines, Delta Air Lines, British Airways, Air Canada, and LIAT offer direct or connecting flights to the islands. Depending on your departure point, flight duration can range from a few hours to a full day.

b. Connecting Flights:

If there are no direct flights available from your location, you can opt for connecting flights. Many travelers fly into major hub airports in the Caribbean, such as San Juan, Puerto Rico (SJU), and then take a short connecting flight to St. Kitts or Nevis. Alternatively, you can fly to neighboring islands, such as Antigua (ANU) or St. Maarten (SXM), and then take a ferry or regional airline to St. Kitts and Nevis.

c. Private Jet:

For those seeking a luxurious and exclusive travel experience, private jet charters are available in St. Kitts and Nevis. The islands have a private jet terminal at the Robert L. Bradshaw International Airport, allowing travelers to arrive in style and enjoy personalized services.

Sea Travel:

While air travel is the most common way to reach St. Kitts and Nevis, sea travel also offers an alternative option. If you prefer a more leisurely journey or are arriving from nearby islands, here's what you need to know about sea travel to St. Kitts and Nevis:

a. Cruise Ships:

St. Kitts and Nevis are popular cruise ship destinations, and many major cruise lines include them in their itineraries. Cruise ships dock at Port Zante in Basseterre, St. Kitts, where passengers can disembark and explore the island. Nevis is also accessible from St. Kitts via a short ferry ride, allowing cruise passengers to experience both islands during their visit.

b. Ferry Services:

Ferry services connect St. Kitts and Nevis with neighboring islands, providing an alternative mode of transportation. The most common ferry route is between Basseterre, St. Kitts, and Charlestown, Nevis. The ferry ride takes approximately 45 minutes and offers stunning views of the Caribbean Sea. Ferry services also connect St. Kitts and Nevis with nearby islands such as Antigua, St. Maarten, and Montserrat.

c. Private Yacht:

For those with access to a private yacht or boat, sailing to St. Kitts and Nevis can be a picturesque and enjoyable experience. The islands have marinas and anchorages where private yachts can dock, providing access to the islands' amenities and attractions.

Considerations for Choosing the Best Option:

When deciding on the best way to move into St. Kitts and Nevis, there are several factors to consider:

a. Time and Convenience:

Air travel is generally faster and more convenient, especially for long-distance journeys. If you're traveling from a distant location or have limited time, flying is likely the best option. Sea travel, on the other hand, offers a more relaxed and scenic journey, allowing you to enjoy the beauty of the Caribbean Sea and visit multiple islands along the way.

b. Cost:

Cost is another important consideration. Air travel can be more expensive, especially during peak travel seasons. However, it offers the advantage of saving time and is often the preferred choice for international travelers. Sea travel, such as ferry services, can be more affordable, particularly for those already in the Caribbean region.

c. Personal Preferences:

Your personal preferences and travel style may also influence your decision. If you enjoy the experience of sailing or prefer a more leisurely journey, sea travel may be the ideal choice. On the other hand, if you prefer the convenience and efficiency of air travel, flying to St. Kitts and Nevis is the way to go.

Planning and Preparation:

Regardless of whether you choose air or sea travel, proper planning and preparation are essential for a smooth journey:

a. Check Travel Restrictions:

Before making any travel arrangements, check the travel restrictions and entry requirements of St. Kitts and Nevis. This includes verifying visa requirements, and passport validity.

b. Book in Advance:

To secure the best deals and availability, it's advisable to book your flights or ferry tickets in advance. This is particularly important during peak travel seasons or if you have specific travel dates in mind.

c. Pack Accordingly:

Consider the specific travel requirements for your chosen mode of transportation. For air travel, adhere to airline regulations regarding baggage allowance and prohibited items. For sea travel, ensure you have the necessary items for a comfortable journey, such as sunscreen, seasickness medication (if needed), and appropriate clothing.

d. Stay Informed:

Stay updated on any changes to flight schedules, ferry services, or travel advisories. Subscribe to travel alerts, follow official sources, and check with airlines or ferry operators for any updates or disruptions that may affect your journey.

Visa Entry Requirement for St. Kitts and Nevis

St. Kitts and Nevis, the enchanting twin-island nation located in the Caribbean, welcomes visitors from around the world to experience its natural beauty, vibrant culture, and warm hospitality. Before planning your trip, it's important to understand the visa entry requirements for St. Kitts and Nevis. In this chapter, I will explore the visa policies, different types of visas available, and the application process, ensuring that you have all the necessary information for a smooth and hassle-free entry into St. Kitts and Nevis.

Visa Exemption:

St. Kitts and Nevis operates a visa exemption policy, allowing citizens of certain countries to enter the islands for tourism or business purposes without a visa. These countries include the United States, Canada, the United Kingdom, most European Union member states, Australia, New Zealand, and many Caribbean countries. Travelers from these countries can stay for up to 90 days without a visa.

Visa-On-Arrival:

For citizens of countries that are not eligible for visa exemption, St. Kitts and Nevis offers a visa-on-arrival facility. Travelers from these countries can obtain a visa upon arrival at the point of entry, such as the Robert L. Bradshaw International Airport or the Vance W. Amory International Airport. The visa-on-arrival allows a stay of up to 30 days and can be extended for an additional 30 days upon application to the Immigration Department.

Visa Requirements:

To enter St. Kitts and Nevis, whether under the visa exemption or visa-on-arrival, travelers must meet certain requirements. These requirements typically include:

a. **Valid Passport**: Travelers must possess a valid passport with a minimum validity of six months beyond the intended departure date from St. Kitts and Nevis.

b. **Return or Onward Ticket:** Proof of a return or onward ticket is required to demonstrate that the traveler intends to leave the country within the permitted duration of stay.

c. **Proof of Accommodation**: Travelers may be asked to provide proof of accommodation, such as hotel reservations or an invitation letter from a host in St. Kitts and Nevis.

d. **Sufficient Funds**: Travelers must have sufficient funds to cover their expenses during their stay in St. Kitts and Nevis. This can be demonstrated through bank statements, cash, or credit cards.

e. **Good Health and Character:** Travelers should be in good health and have no criminal record or history of visa violations. Immigration officers have the discretion to deny entry to individuals who pose a security risk or have previously violated immigration laws.

Visa Extensions:

If you wish to extend your stay beyond the permitted duration, you can apply for a visa extension through the Immigration Department in St. Kitts and Nevis. The extension is granted based on the discretion of the immigration authorities and is subject to certain conditions. It's advisable to apply for an extension well in advance of your authorized stay to avoid any legal complications.

Work and Residency Permits:

If you intend to work or reside in St. Kitts and Nevis for an extended period, you will need to apply for the appropriate work or residency permit. These permits have specific requirements, including proof of employment, investment in the country, or close family ties to St. Kitts and Nevis. It's recommended to consult with the Immigration Department or seek professional advice to understand the process and requirements for obtaining work or residency permits.

Visa Application Process:

If you are not eligible for visa exemption or visa-on-arrival, you will need to apply for a visa through the nearest St. Kitts and Nevis embassy or consulate. The visa application process typically involves the following steps:

a. **Obtain the Application Form**: Download the visa application form from the official website of the embassy or consulate or collect it in person.

b. **Complete the Application Form**: Fill in the required details accurately and provide all the necessary supporting documents as specified by the embassy or consulate.

c. **Submit the Application**: Submit the completed application form and supporting documents to the embassy or consulate along with the applicable visa fee. Some embassies or consulates may require an in-person interview as part of the application process.

d. **Processing Time**: The processing time for visa applications can vary depending on the embassy or consulate and other factors. It's advisable to apply well in advance of your intended travel dates to allow sufficient processing time.

e. **Visa Collection**: Once your visa application is approved, you can collect your visa from the embassy or consulate. Check the specific instructions provided by the embassy or consulate for visa collection procedures.

It's important to note that visa requirements and processes may change, and it's recommended to check the official website of the St. Kitts and Nevis embassy or consulate in your country for the most up-to-date information.

List of Countries Exempt in St. Kitts and Nevis

The government of St. Kitts and Nevis has implemented a visa exemption policy, allowing citizens of certain countries to enter the islands for tourism or business purposes without a visa. In this chapter, I will provide an extensive list of countries exempt from visa requirements in St. Kitts and Nevis, ensuring that you have all the necessary information for a hassle-free visit.

It's important to note that visa exemption policies can change, and it's advisable to check the official website of St. Kitts and Nevis embassy or consulate in your country for the most up-to-date information. Here is a list of countries that are currently exempt from visa requirements in St. Kitts and Nevis:

North America:

United States: Citizens of the United States are exempt from visa requirements and can stay in St. Kitts and Nevis for up to 90 days.

Canada: Canadian citizens can enter St. Kitts and Nevis without a visa and stay for up to 90 days.

European Union:

United Kingdom: Citizens of the United Kingdom, including British Overseas Territories citizens with a valid passport, are visa-exempt for a stay of up to 90 days.

Germany, France, Italy, Spain, Netherlands, Sweden, Denmark, Austria, Finland, Belgium, Portugal, Greece, Luxembourg, Ireland, Malta, Cyprus, Estonia, Latvia, Lithuania, Slovakia, Slovenia, Hungary, Czech Republic, Poland, Romania, Bulgaria: Citizens of these European Union member states can enter St. Kitts and Nevis without a visa and stay for up to 90 days.

Caribbean:

Antigua and Barbuda: Citizens of Antigua and Barbuda are exempt from visa requirements and can stay in St. Kitts and Nevis for up to 90 days.

- **Barbados**: Barbadian citizens can enter St. Kitts and Nevis without a visa and stay for up to 90 days.

- **Dominica:** Citizens of Dominica are visa-exempt and can stay in St. Kitts and Nevis for up to 90 days.
- **Grenada:** Grenadian citizens can enter St. Kitts and Nevis without a visa and stay for up to 90 days.
- **St. Lucia:** Citizens of St. Lucia are exempt from visa requirements and can stay in St. Kitts and Nevis for up to 90 days.
- **St. Vincent and the Grenadines:** Citizens of St. Vincent and the Grenadines can enter St. Kitts and Nevis without a visa and stay for up to 90 days.

Other Countries:

- **Australia**: Australian citizens are visa-exempt and can stay in St. Kitts and Nevis for up to 90 days.
- **New Zealand**: Citizens of New Zealand can enter St. Kitts and Nevis without a visa and stay for up to 90 days.

It's important to note that the duration of stay for visa-exempt countries is typically up to 90 days. If you wish to extend your stay beyond this period, you may need to apply for a visa extension through the Immigration Department in St. Kitts and Nevis.

While the above list includes the most common countries exempt from visa requirements in St. Kitts and Nevis, there may be additional countries not mentioned. It's always recommended to check the official website of the St. Kitts and Nevis embassy or consulate in your country for the most up-to-date and accurate information regarding visa requirements.

List of Countries that are NOT Visa Exempt

While citizens of many nations are exempt from needing a visa to visit St. Kitts and Nevis, citizens of some nations are required to obtain one before visiting the islands. I will provide a comprehensive list of countries that do not require a visa for St. Kitts and Nevis in this comprehensive guide to make sure you have all the information you need to plan your trip.

It's important to remember that visa policies can change, so the most up-to-date information can be found on the official website of the St. Kitts and Nevis embassy or consulate in your country. The following countries do not currently require St. Kitts and Nevis to have a visa:

African nations:

Algeria, Angola, Burundi, Cameroon, Central African Republic, Chad, Comoros, Congo (Democratic Republic) Congo (Republic), Cote d'Ivoire (Ivory Coast), Djibouti Egypt, Equatorial, Guinea, Eritrea, Ethiopia, Gabon, Gambia, Ghana, Guinea, Guinea-Bissau, Kenya, Lesotho,

Liberia, Libya, Madagascar, Malawi, Mali, Mauritania, Mauritius, Morocco, Mozambique, Namibia, Niger, Nigeria, Rwanda, Sao Tome and Principe Senegal Sierra

- Afghanistan
- Bangladesh
- Bhutan
- China
- India
- Iran
- Iraq
- North Korea
- Pakistan
- Saudi Arabia
- Sri Lanka
- Syria
- Yemen
- Center Eastern Nations:
- Bahrain
- Kuwait
- Lebanon
- Oman
- Qatar
- Joined Bedouin Emirates

South American Nations:

Other nations include; Argentina, Bolivia, Brazil, Chile, Colombia, Ecuador, Guyana, Paraguay, Suriname, Uruguay, and Venezuela.

- Russia
- Belarus
- Kazakhstan
- Uzbekistan
- Turkmenistan
- Mongolia
- Kyrgyzstan

Residents of the previously mentioned nations are expected to get a visa before going to St. Kitts and Nevis. The visa application process normally includes presenting an application structure, supporting reports, and paying the relevant visa expense at the closest St. Kitts and Nevis international haven or department in their nation of home. It's essential to adhere to the particular guidelines given by the government office or department and permit adequate time for visa handling.

Although the most common nations that do not require a visa for St. Kitts and Nevis are included on this list, it is possible that additional nations are not mentioned. The most up-to-date and accurate information regarding visa requirements can always be found on the official website of St. Kitts and Nevis embassy or consulate in your country.

My Personal Combo to get the Most out of St. Kitts

Exploring Basseterre - The Capital City

On the island of St. Kitts, Basseterre, the capital city of St. Kitts and Nevis, is a vibrant and historic destination. With its rich social legacy, enchanting provincial design, and clamoring climate, Basseterre offers a huge number of attractions and encounters for guests to investigate. I will take a comprehensive look at the highlights of Basseterre to ensure that you have all the information you need to make the most of your visit to this captivating capital city.

Historical Significance:

Basseterre has a long history, going back to the 17th century. Visit Independence Square, the city's heart and a significant historical site, to begin your exploration. The Berkeley Memorial Clock, a prominent landmark honoring the emancipation of African slaves, can be found here. The St. George's Anglican Church, one of the Caribbean's oldest churches, and the National Museum, which displays the island's history and cultural artifacts, are nearby attractions.

The Circus:

The Bazaar, motivated by London's Piccadilly Carnival, is a clamoring indirect in the focal point of Basseterre. This notable milestone is encircled by pleasant Georgian-style structures with beguiling verandas. Admire the architecture and the vibrant shops, boutiques, and local vendors that offer one-of-a-kind souvenirs and handicrafts as you take a stroll around the Circus.

Independence Square:

Independence Square, which is in the center of Basseterre, is not only a historical landmark but also a lively gathering spot for both locals and visitors. Relax on one of the benches, take in the vibrant atmosphere, and watch the world go by. In addition, throughout the year, the square plays host to several festivals and events that provide a glimpse into the cultural life of St. Kitts and Nevis.

Fort George:

Go to Fort George for sweeping vistas of Basseterre and the surrounding area. The city and the Caribbean Sea can be seen from this historic fort, which is perched atop a hill. Investigate the post's defenses, cannons, and underground passages while finding out about the island's frontier past. Remember to carry your camera to catch the stunning vistas.

Shopping and Dining:

Basseterre is home to a plethora of boutiques, craft markets, and duty-free shops, all of which contribute to the city's vivacious retail scene. Peruse the bright slows down at Port Zante or visit the Pelican Shopping Center for a blend of neighborhood and worldwide brands. The city provides a wide range of dining options, ranging from regional Caribbean fare to international flavors. Test new fish, enjoy genuine West Indian dishes, or relish global rarities at the city's assorted eateries and road food slows down.

St. Kitts Scenic Railway:

Take a thrilling ride along the St. Kitts coastline on the St. Kitts Scenic Railway for an unforgettable experience. The island's picturesque villages, stunning beaches, and lush landscapes can all be seen from this narrow-gauge train. Enjoy a refreshing beverage while taking a break in one of the train's observation cars while taking in the live commentary that provides insight into the island's history and culture.

Beaches:

The pristine beaches that surround Basseterre are an essential part of any trip. Beautiful sandy shores, crystal-clear waters, and a variety of water sports are all within easy reach of the city center. Whether you incline toward relaxing on the oceanfront, swimming, or taking a stab at water sports, the seashores close to Basseterre offer a cut of heaven for unwinding and experiencing.

Brimstone Hill Fortress National Park:

While not in Basseterre, a visit to St. Kitts is fragmented without investigating the Brimstone Slope Stronghold Public Park. This UNESCO World Legacy Site is found close to the capital and is a demonstration of the island's pilgrim past. Investigate the very much-safeguarded fortresses, stroll along the defenses, and find out about the essential meaning of this noteworthy site. The all-encompassing perspectives from the fort are genuinely amazing.

Brimstone Hill Fortress National Park

On the Caribbean island of St. Kitts, Brimstone Hill Fortress National Park is a remarkable historical site that offers a captivating journey into the island's rich past. The well-preserved fortifications, stunning views, and immersive historical experience of this UNESCO World Heritage Site are well-known. In this far-reaching guide, we will dig into the subtleties of Brimstone Slope Fortification Public Park, revealing insight into its set of experiences, importance, and the remarkable encounters it offers to guests.

Historical Significance:

The impressive Brimstone Hill Fortress, also known as "The Gibraltar of the West Indies," is a reminder of the island's colonial past. Built by the English in the late seventeenth 100 years, the fortification filled in as an essential safeguard post against rival European powers and assumed a significant part in safeguarding the important sugar estates of St. Kitts.

Architecture and Design:

The fortress is a masterpiece of architecture that combines stunning natural settings with military technology. The historical struggle for dominance between the two colonial powers in the Caribbean is reflected in its unique design, which incorporates a fusion of British and French styles. The impressive stone walls, bastions, and gun emplacements demonstrate the time's cutting-edge defenses.

Fortifications and Structures:

The Brimstone Hill Fortress is made up of several structures that are linked together and once formed a complicated defense system. Investigate the very much protected defenses, investigate the organization of passages, and stroll along the procession ground to acquire a feeling of the stronghold's scale and vital importance. The Stronghold, the most elevated mark of the post, offers all-encompassing perspectives on the encompassing scenes and the Caribbean Ocean.

Museum and Interpretive Center:

The Brimstone Hill Fortress National Park Museum and Interpretive Center are open to visitors who visit the park. The gallery gives top-to-bottom bits of knowledge into the set of experiences, design, and meaning of the fortification through shows, curios, and enlightening showcases. Learn about the soldiers' lives, the effects of colonialism, and St. Kitts and Nevis's cultural heritage.

Scenic Views:

One of the features of visiting Brimstone Slope Fort Public Park is the amazing all-encompassing perspectives it offers. You can take in the surrounding islands, their sparkling Caribbean Sea, and the lush green landscapes from the elevated vantage points. The perspectives are especially dazzling during dawn or nightfall, projecting a warm brilliant shine over the fort and its environmental elements.

Walking Trails:

The park has well-kept walking trails that let people see the area's natural beauty and learn about its historical significance. Enjoy the peace of the area as you stroll along the paths, surrounded by tropical plants and animals. Interpretive signage along the paths gives significant data about the greenery, fauna, and history of the area.

Cultural Events and Festivals:

Brimstone Hill Fortress National Park hosts a variety of cultural events and festivals that highlight the heritage and history of St. Kitts and Nevis throughout the year. From live concerts and verifiable reenactments to workmanship presentations and instructive projects, these occasions give a vivid and intelligent experience for guests.

Visitor Facilities:

To enhance the visitor experience, the park provides a variety of facilities. Picnic areas, a gift shop, a visitor center, and restrooms are among these. For those who want to learn more about the fortress's history and significance, guided tours are available.

Accessibility:

Every visitor is welcome at Brimstone Hill Fortress National Park. Despite the difficulties posed by the historic nature of the location, efforts have been made to make it accessible to people with disabilities. To ensure that everyone can appreciate the fortress's beauty and history, accessible walkways, ramps, and viewing areas are available.

Beaches and Water Activities

The islands of St. Kitts and Nevis, which are located in the center of the Caribbean, are well-known for their clean beaches, crystal-clear waters, and numerous exciting water sports. With their pleasant shorelines, these sister islands offer a heaven for ocean-side darlings and water devotees. In this thorough aid, we will investigate the dazzling sea shores and exciting water exercises that anticipate guests in St. Kitts and Nevis.

Frigate Bay Beach:

Frigate Sound Ocean side, situated on the southeastern bank of St. Kitts, is a well-known objective for the two vacationers and local people. The golden sand on the beach is stunning, and the turquoise water gently laps it. Take a cool dip in the Caribbean Sea, unwind under the swaying palm trees, and enjoy the sun. In addition, Frigate Bay Beach is home to several beachfront bars and restaurants where you can enjoy tropical drinks and local fare.

Pinney's Beach:

Pinney's Beach, a long stretch of pristine white sand that is frequently regarded as one of the Caribbean's most beautiful beaches, can be found on the neighboring island of Nevis. There are charming beach bars and restaurants all along this idyllic beach, where you can savor a delicious meal while taking in the expansive views of the sea. Take a stroll along the shore, go swimming, or just take in the scenery's beauty.

Cockleshell Beach:

On the southern tip of St. Kitts, Cockleshell Beach offers a serene and picturesque setting. With its delicate sands, quiet waters, and stunning perspectives on Nevis across the Strait, this ocean side is a shelter for unwinding. Loosen up on an ocean-side lounger, swim free waters to find dynamic marine life, or partake in a beachside rub for a definitive spoiling experience.

South Friars Beach:

On the southern coast of St. Kitts, South Friars Beach is a treasure trove that is hard to find. This detached and tranquil ocean side is encircled by rich vegetation, making a tropical heaven air. Relax on the clean sands, go swimming in the calm waters, or go snorkeling to see the vibrant coral reefs just off the shore. Additionally, there are beach bars and restaurants where you can sample local cuisine and sip a cool drink.

Water Activities:

Adventure seekers can choose from a wide range of thrilling water sports in St. Kitts and Nevis. There is something for everyone to enjoy, from kayaking and paddleboarding to snorkeling and scuba diving. Swim with tropical fish, explore the vibrant underwater world, and marvel at the diverse coral reefs. You can likewise take a stab at stream skiing, parasailing, or remote ocean looking for a more adrenaline-siphoning experience. The islands' warm, crystal-clear waters are the ideal setting for water sports.

Catamaran Cruises:

Leave on a sailboat journey to investigate the excellence of St. Kitts and Nevis according to an alternate point of view. Sail along the shorelines, partaking in the dazzling perspectives, and halting at beautiful bays and disconnected sea shores en route. Enjoy a sumptuous onboard meal, snorkel in crystal-clear waters, and soak up the sun on the ample decks of the catamaran.

Boat Trips to Nevis:

Go on a boat outing from St. Kitts to its sister island, Nevis, for a day of investigation and unwinding. Disembark in Nevis to explore its pristine beaches, historic landmarks, and charming villages after a scenic journey across the turquoise waters. Enjoy a spa treatment at one of Nevis' opulent resorts, explore historical sites like the birthplace of Alexander Hamilton, or unwind on the beach.

Sunset Cruises:

Take a romantic cruise at sunset to cap off your day in paradise. Sail along the shorelines of St. Kitts and Nevis as the sun paints the sky with energetic tones. As you take in the splendor of the Caribbean sunset and nibble on delectable hors d'oeuvres, sip champagne. This is a remarkable encounter that will make enduring recollections.

Rainforest Hiking and Nature Trails

The rainforest climbing and nature trails in St. Kitts and Nevis offer an exceptional chance to interface with nature, investigate different environments, and witness the magnificence of the Caribbean's greenery. There is a hike for everyone, from strolls through botanical gardens to strenuous ascents of volcanic peaks. In this chapter, we will dig into the subtleties of rainforest climbing and nature trails in St. Kitts and Nevis, displaying the different environments and one-of-a-kind encounters that anticipate pioneers.

Central Forest Reserve:

The Central Forest Reserve, located in St. Kitts, is a protected area that covers a significant portion of the island's interior. This rainforest paradise is home to a rich variety of plant and animal species, making it a haven for nature lovers. Explore the network of well-maintained trails that wind through the reserve, offering a chance to witness the beauty of towering trees, vibrant flowers, and the songs of tropical birds. Keep an eye out for the native Green

Vervet monkeys, which are commonly spotted swinging through the trees.

Mount Liamuiga:

For those seeking a more challenging hiking adventure, a trek up Mount Liamuiga is a must. Rising to an impressive height of 3,792 feet, this dormant volcano dominates the landscape of St. Kitts. The hike to the summit takes you through lush rainforests, volcanic rock formations, and eventually rewards you with panoramic views of the surrounding islands and the Caribbean Sea. It is recommended to embark on this hike with a knowledgeable guide who can provide insight into the geology, flora, and fauna of the area.

Nevis Peak:

On the sister island of Nevis, nature enthusiasts can conquer Nevis Peak, the island's highest point. This challenging hike takes you through dense rainforest, steep slopes, and rocky terrain, rewarding you with breathtaking vistas from the summit. The trail is marked by the ruins of the old sugar plantations, providing glimpses into the island's history. As you ascend, you'll be surrounded by a lush ecosystem teeming with tropical plants, exotic birds, and the occasional glimpse of wildlife.

Botanical Gardens:

For those who prefer a more leisurely nature experience, the botanical gardens in St. Kitts and Nevis offer an enchanting escape. The gardens are meticulously maintained, showcasing a vast collection of tropical plants, colorful flowers, and exotic species. Take a peaceful stroll through the well-manicured paths, breathe in the fragrant scents of the flowers, and admire the vibrant displays of nature's beauty. The gardens also serve as educational centers, offering insights into the diverse flora and fauna of the islands.

Wingfield Estate:

The Wingfield Estate, located in St. Kitts, is not only historically significant but also boasts beautiful nature trails that wind through the surrounding rainforest. Explore the remnants of the estate, including the old sugar mill, ruins, and lush gardens. The trails offer a chance to observe the native wildlife, including birds, butterflies, and small mammals. Guided tours are available, providing historical and ecological information about the area.

Eco-Lodges and Nature Retreats:

For a truly immersive rainforest experience, consider staying at one of the eco-lodges or nature retreats in St. Kitts and Nevis. These accommodations are nestled within or near the rainforest, offering a unique opportunity to wake up to the sounds of nature and embark on guided hikes and nature walks. Immerse yourself in the tranquil ambiance, learn about the local ecology, and embrace the serenity of the rainforest.

Bird Watching:

St. Kitts and Nevis are a haven for bird watchers, as the islands are home to a wide variety of bird species. The rainforest trails provide excellent opportunities to spot colorful birds such as the St. Kitts Parrot, Bananaquit, and the Lesser Antillean Bullfinch. Bring along a pair of binoculars and a birding guidebook to enhance your bird-watching experience.

Responsible Hiking:

While exploring the rainforest trails, it is essential to practice responsible hiking. Respect the natural environment by staying on designated trails, avoiding littering, and refraining from disturbing the wildlife. It is also advisable to wear appropriate footwear, carry sufficient water, and apply insect repellent to ensure a safe and comfortable hiking experience.

My Top 7 Notable Festivals and Cultural Events to Attend

Attending these notable festivals and cultural events in St. Kitts and Nevis offers a unique opportunity to immerse yourself in the rich heritage, vibrant traditions, and lively atmosphere of the islands. From the pulsating rhythms of the St. Kitts Music Festival to the colorful parades of the National Carnival, each event showcases the cultural diversity and artistic talents of the local community. Experience the warmth of the Caribbean hospitality, indulge in the flavors of local cuisine, and create lasting memories as you celebrate alongside the vibrant people of St. Kitts and Nevis.

1. St. Kitts Music Festival:

The St. Kitts Music Festival is a vibrant celebration of music that takes place annually in June. This three-day event brings together local and international artists who perform a diverse range of musical genres, including reggae, soca, calypso, R&B, and jazz. The festival attracts music enthusiasts from around the world, creating an energetic atmosphere filled with infectious rhythms and captivating performances. It's an excellent opportunity to immerse yourself in the rich musical heritage of St. Kitts and enjoy world-class entertainment.

2. Culturama (Nevis):

Culturama is a colorful and lively cultural festival held on the island of Nevis in late July or early August. The festival showcases the vibrant traditions, arts, and music of the island. The week-long celebration includes parades, street dances, calypso competitions, beauty pageants, and traditional cultural performances. Experience the vibrant costumes, taste the local cuisine, and join in the lively festivities as the island comes alive with cultural pride and excitement.

3. Nevis Mango & Food Festival:

The Nevis Mango & Food Festival is a culinary extravaganza that celebrates the island's delectable mangoes and local cuisine. Held in July, this festival offers a unique opportunity to indulge in mango-inspired dishes prepared by renowned local and international chefs. From mango-infused cocktails to mango-themed cooking demonstrations, the festival showcases the versatility and deliciousness of this tropical fruit. Enjoy live music, sample mouthwatering dishes, and savor the flavors of Nevis in a festive and relaxed setting.

4. St. Kitts and Nevis National Carnival:

The St. Kitts and Nevis National Carnival, also known as Sugar Mas, is the pinnacle of cultural celebrations in the country. Spanning several weeks from December to January, this carnival is a riot of color, music, and revelry. It features a series of events, including parades, calypso competitions, beauty pageants, J'ouvert (a street party), and masquerade performances. Experience the infectious energy, marvel at the elaborate costumes, dance to the pulsating soca rhythms, and immerse yourself in the vibrant carnival spirit.

5. Easterama (St. Kitts):

Easterama is a traditional Easter festival celebrated on the island of St. Kitts. It combines religious observances with cultural performances and entertainment. The festival features a grand parade showcasing local talent, music, and dance. Enjoy the lively street performances, watch the traditional Bull and Donkey Dance, and partake in the festive atmosphere as the island commemorates Easter with a blend of faith and cultural festivities.

6. Green Valley Festival (Nevis):

The Green Valley Festival is a unique celebration of the heritage and traditions of the village of Gingerland in Nevis. Held annually in August, the festival showcases the vibrant culture and history of the community. Enjoy the street parades, cultural shows, traditional music and dance performances, and local food stalls. The festival provides a glimpse into the rural traditions of Nevis and offers an opportunity to engage with the local community.

7. Emancipation Day:

Emancipation Day is a significant cultural event that commemorates the abolition of slavery in St. Kitts and Nevis. Celebrated on August 1st, it is a day of reflection, remembrance, and cultural activities. The day begins with a traditional sunrise service, followed by parades, cultural performances, and exhibitions. Learn about the history of slavery, participate in discussions and lectures, and join in the festivities as the nation honors its journey towards freedom.

Shopping and Souvenirs

St. Kitts and Nevis are home to a vibrant shopping scene where visitors can find unique souvenirs, local crafts, and a variety of goods to take home as mementos of their trip. Whether you're looking for traditional handicrafts, local artwork, or duty-free luxury items, there are plenty of options to explore. In this section, I will delve into the shopping experiences and popular souvenirs that await you in St. Kitts and Nevis.

Port Zante:

Located in the capital city of Basseterre, Port Zante is a popular shopping hub for tourists. Here you'll find an array of duty-free shops offering jewelry, watches, perfumes, and designer clothing. The area is known for its high-end brands and luxury items, making it a haven for fashion enthusiasts and those seeking upscale souvenirs. Take your time to browse through the stores, compare prices, and find that perfect item to take home.

Caribelle Batik:

A visit to Caribelle Batik is a must for those seeking unique and locally crafted souvenirs. Located at Romney Manor in St. Kitts, this historic site is home to a workshop where artisans create beautiful batik textiles. Watch the fascinating batik-making process, which involves hand-dyeing and wax-resistant techniques, and browse through a wide selection of clothing, accessories, and home décor items. Each piece is a work of art, showcasing vibrant colors and intricate designs inspired by the Caribbean culture and nature.

Craft Fairs and Markets:

Exploring the local craft fairs and markets is an excellent way to discover authentic souvenirs and support local artisans. The Pelican Mall Craft Market in Basseterre is a popular spot where you can find a variety of handmade crafts, including wood carvings, straw baskets, pottery, and jewelry. The market is a lively and bustling place, filled with friendly vendors eager to share their stories and showcase their creations.

Art Galleries:

For art enthusiasts, St. Kitts and Nevis are home to several art galleries where you can admire and purchase local artwork. The National Museum in Basseterre features a collection of artwork and historical artifacts, providing a glimpse into the cultural heritage of the islands. The Nevis Artisan Village in Charlestown, Nevis, is another notable location where you can find a diverse range of artwork, including paintings, sculptures, and ceramics created by local artists.

Local Delicacies and Products:

When it comes to souvenirs, don't forget to explore the culinary delights and local products of St. Kitts and Nevis. The islands are known for their rum production, so consider bringing back a bottle of locally distilled rum as a unique gift. You can also find an assortment of delicious treats such as jams, hot sauces, and spices made from local fruits and spices. These items are not only great for your own enjoyment but also make for excellent gifts for friends and family back home.

Duty-Free Shopping:

St. Kitts and Nevis are known for their duty-free shopping, offering visitors the opportunity to purchase luxury items at discounted prices. The Port Zante shopping area and the resort areas are particularly popular for duty-free shopping. Look out for watches, jewelry, electronics, and designer clothing from renowned brands. Keep in mind that you may need to show your passport and travel documents to take advantage of the duty-free prices.

Local Fashion and Clothing:

If you're interested in local fashion and clothing, look for boutiques and shops that specialize in Caribbean-inspired designs. You can find unique pieces made from colorful fabrics and prints, reflecting the vibrant culture of the islands. From dresses and shirts to swimwear and accessories, these items will not only remind you of your trip but also allow you to showcase a bit of Caribbean flair in your wardrobe.

When shopping in St. Kitts and Nevis, remember to explore different areas, compare prices, and engage with the locals. Bargaining is not typically practiced in the formal stores, but you may have some room for negotiation at craft markets. Additionally, be aware of any restrictions on importing certain items to your home country and inquire about the necessary paperwork or permits if purchasing protected wildlife or cultural artifacts.

This page was left blank intentionally

My Personal Combo to get the Most out of Nevis

Exploring Charlestown - The Main Town

Charlestown, the charming main town of the island of Nevis, offers visitors a glimpse into the rich history and laid-back charm of the Caribbean. With its quaint streets, historic buildings, and picturesque waterfront, Charlestown exudes a unique character that invites exploration. In this chapter, I will take you on a journey through the highlights and must-see attractions of this enchanting town.

The Alexander Hamilton Museum:

Begin your exploration of Charlestown at the Alexander Hamilton Museum, located in the birthplace of the renowned founding father. Housed in a beautifully restored Georgian-style building, the museum offers a fascinating insight into the life and achievements of Alexander Hamilton. Explore the exhibits that showcase his early years on Nevis, his rise to prominence in the United States, and his enduring legacy. It's a must-visit for history buffs and anyone interested in the life of this influential figure.

Charlestown Waterfront:

Take a leisurely stroll along the Charlestown Waterfront and soak in the scenic beauty of the harbor. Admire the colorful boats bobbing in the clear turquoise waters and enjoy the gentle breeze. The waterfront is lined with charming historic buildings, including the Old Treasury Building and the Bath Hotel, which add to the town's colonial charm. Pause to relax on one of the benches or find a spot at a waterfront café and savor the peaceful ambiance.

The Museum of Nevis History:

Continue your journey through Charlestown's history at the Museum of Nevis History. Housed in a restored 18th-century Georgian building, this museum offers a comprehensive overview of the island's past. Explore the exhibits that cover various aspects of Nevisian history, including the indigenous Carib population, colonial-era plantations, the sugar industry, and the abolition of slavery.

The museum also pays tribute to other notable Nevisians, such as Lord Nelson and the famed writer, C.S. Lewis.

Charlestown Market:

Immerse yourself in the local culture and vibrant atmosphere by visiting the Charlestown Market. Located in the heart of town, this bustling market is the perfect place to experience the vibrant colors, flavors, and aromas of Nevis. Browse through stalls selling fresh fruits, vegetables, spices, and local handicrafts. Engage with the friendly vendors, sample some of the local delicacies, and perhaps pick up some souvenirs to take home.

Bath Hotel and Spring House:

A short distance from Charlestown, you'll find the historic Bath Hotel and Spring House. Built in 1778, this former luxury hotel was frequented by European aristocracy and notable figures of the time, seeking the therapeutic benefits of the natural hot springs. Although the hotel is no longer operational, visitors can still tour the grounds and learn about the history of this grand establishment. Take a dip in the mineral-rich waters and rejuvenate yourself as people have done for centuries.

Nevis Court House:

The Nevis Court House is another architectural gem worth visiting in Charlestown. Built in 1825, this imposing structure is a prominent landmark in the town. Admire its neoclassical design, with its distinctive clock tower and grand entrance. The Court House is still in use today, adding a sense of history and significance to the town's administration.

Charlestown Churches:

Charlestown is home to several historic churches, each with its own unique character and significance. The St. Paul's Anglican Church, with its striking white exterior and neoclassical architecture, is one of the oldest churches in the Caribbean. The St. Thomas' Anglican Church, known for its beautiful stained glass windows, is another notable place of worship in the town. Take the time to visit these churches, appreciate their architectural beauty, and experience the serenity within their walls.

Dining and Shopping:

Charlestown offers a range of dining options, from local eateries serving authentic Caribbean cuisine to upscale restaurants offering international flavors. Indulge in fresh seafood, local delicacies, and tantalizing flavors that reflect the island's culinary heritage. Afterward, explore the town's boutique shops and art galleries, where you can find unique souvenirs, local crafts, and artwork.

Nevis Peak and Nature Reserves

Nevis, the tranquil and lush island in the Caribbean, is not only known for its pristine beaches and charming towns but also for its breathtaking natural landscapes. At the heart of the island stands Nevis Peak, a dormant volcano that dominates the skyline and offers adventurous travelers the opportunity to embark on an unforgettable hiking experience. Surrounding the peak are nature reserves and protected areas that preserve the island's unique flora and fauna. In this detailed guide, we will explore Nevis Peak and the nature reserves, highlighting their natural beauty and the activities they offer.

Nevis Peak:

Nevis Peak, standing at an impressive 3,232 feet (985 meters), is the centerpiece of the island's natural beauty. It is a challenging yet rewarding hike for outdoor enthusiasts and nature lovers. The trail to the summit takes you through lush rainforests, up steep slopes, and offers breathtaking panoramic views as you ascend. The hike is best undertaken with an experienced guide who can navigate the terrain and provide insights into the flora, fauna, and history of the area. The ascent can be demanding, but reaching the summit and soaking in the awe-inspiring vistas of Nevis and the neighboring islands is truly a memorable experience.

Central Forest Reserve:

The Central Forest Reserve, located on the slopes of Nevis Peak, is a protected area that encompasses approximately 1,000 acres of dense rainforest. It is home to a diverse range of plant and animal species, including tropical birds, monkeys, and exotic flora. Guided tours through the reserve allow visitors to explore the lush vegetation, listen to the sounds of the forest, and learn about the ecological importance of preserving this pristine habitat. The reserve also offers picnic areas and nature trails for visitors to enjoy a leisurely walk and immerse themselves in the tranquility of nature.

The Botanical Gardens of Nevis:

For those seeking a more curated nature experience, a visit to the Botanical Gardens of Nevis is a must. Located in the Montpelier Estate, these beautiful gardens showcase a stunning collection of tropical plants, flowers, and trees. Stroll through the manicured lawns, discover hidden pathways, and admire the vibrant colors and fragrances of the botanical wonders. The gardens also feature a tropical rainforest conservatory, home to a variety of exotic bird species. It's an ideal place to relax, rejuvenate, and reconnect with nature.

Nelson Spring Nature Trail:

The Nelson Spring Nature Trail offers visitors a guided tour through the rainforest, providing an immersive experience in Nevis' natural beauty. This trail, located near the village of Gingerland, meanders through lush foliage, across bubbling streams, and past ancient ruins. Along the way, knowledgeable guides share insights into the flora and fauna, as well as the historical significance of the area. The highlight of the trail is a refreshing dip in a natural spring, where you can cool off and rejuvenate amidst the serenity of the forest.

Jonny Cake Trail:

For a shorter but equally rewarding hike, consider the Jonny Cake Trail. This trail takes you through the northeastern part of Nevis, offering stunning views of the coastline, neighboring islands, and the lush greenery that covers the landscape. The trail is named after the traditional Caribbean snack known as "jonny cake" and provides an opportunity to learn about the island's culinary heritage while enjoying the picturesque surroundings.

Bird Watching:

Nevis is a haven for birdwatchers, with over 150 species of birds recorded on the island. The diverse habitats, including rainforests, wetlands, and coastal areas, attract a wide variety of avian species. Birdwatching enthusiasts can spot colorful birds such as the Antillean crested hummingbird, red-billed tropicbird, and bananaquit, among others. The Central Forest Reserve and the Botanical Gardens of Nevis are particularly popular spots for birdwatching, as they provide opportunities to observe both resident and migratory species in their natural habitats.

My Top 10 Beautiful Beaches and Water Sports You Must See

St. Kitts and Nevis are blessed with a plethora of beautiful beaches and exciting water sports activities. From the lively atmosphere of Frigate Bay Beach to the tranquil serenity of Lover's Beach, each destination offers its unique charm and opportunities for relaxation and adventure. Whether you're a sunseeker, a water sports enthusiast, or a nature lover, you'll find the perfect beach and water sports experience in this stunning Caribbean paradise. So pack your swimsuit, sunscreen, and sense of adventure, and get ready to explore the breathtaking beaches and dive into the vibrant underwater world of St. Kitts and Nevis. Here's a detailed guide to my top 10 beautiful beaches and water sports you must see in St. Kitts and Nevis:

1. Frigate Bay Beach (St. Kitts):

Frigate Bay Beach is a popular destination known for its stunning golden sands and crystal-clear waters. Located on the southeastern peninsula of St. Kitts, it offers a range of water sports activities such as snorkeling, jet skiing, and paddleboarding. The beach is lined with beach bars and restaurants, providing convenient access to refreshments and delicious Caribbean cuisine. Frigate Bay Beach is an ideal spot to relax, soak up the sun, and enjoy the lively beach atmosphere.

2. Pinney's Beach (Nevis):

Pinney's Beach, located on the western coast of Nevis, is a breathtaking stretch of white sand that stretches for miles. The beach offers a tranquil and serene setting, perfect for sunbathing and enjoying the crystal-clear waters. Water sports enthusiasts can partake in activities such as kayaking, windsurfing, and kiteboarding. The beach is also home to several beachfront restaurants and bars, where you can indulge in delectable seafood dishes and refreshing tropical drinks.

3. South Friars Beach (St. Kitts):

South Friars Beach is a hidden gem located on the southern coast of St. Kitts. It offers a more secluded and peaceful beach experience, away from the crowds. The calm waters make it an ideal spot for swimming, snorkeling, and stand-up paddleboarding. The beach is fringed with lush vegetation, providing shade for those seeking a break from the sun. Facilities such as beach chairs, umbrellas, and beach bars are available for visitors' convenience.

4. Oualie Beach (Nevis):

Oualie Beach, situated on the northern coast of Nevis, is a picturesque beach with powdery white sand and clear turquoise waters. It is known for its tranquil ambiance and stunning views of neighboring St. Kitts. Water sports enthusiasts can enjoy activities such as sailing, kayaking, and snorkeling, while nature lovers can explore the nearby coral reefs and marine life. The beach is home to a beachfront hotel and restaurant, offering comfortable amenities and delicious Caribbean cuisine.

5. Cockleshell Bay (St. Kitts):

Cockleshell Bay is a pristine beach located on the southeastern tip of St. Kitts, offering breathtaking views of Nevis across the Narrows. The beach is known for its calm waters, making it perfect for swimming and snorkeling. Water sports enthusiasts can also indulge in activities such as jet skiing and parasailing. Cockleshell Bay is home to several beach bars and restaurants, where you can savor local delicacies and enjoy refreshing tropical drinks while lounging on the beach.

6. Lover's Beach (Nevis):

Lover's Beach is a secluded and romantic spot nestled between the hills on the northern coast of Nevis. Accessible only by boat or a short hike, it offers a serene and intimate beach experience. The crystal-clear waters and pristine sands make it an idyllic setting for swimming and sunbathing. Visitors can also explore the surrounding coral reefs and enjoy snorkeling in the vibrant underwater world. Lover's Beach is an excellent choice for couples seeking privacy and tranquility.

7. North Friars Beach (St. Kitts):

North Friars Beach, located on the northern coast of St. Kitts, is a picturesque stretch of golden sand with calm waters and a relaxed atmosphere. The beach offers excellent conditions for swimming, snorkeling, and paddleboarding. Visitors can rent beach chairs and umbrellas for a comfortable day by the sea or indulge in beachfront dining at the nearby restaurants. North Friars Beach is also a popular spot for watching the magnificent sunset over the Caribbean Sea.

8. Sandy Bank Bay (Nevis):

Sandy Bank Bay, situated on the northwestern coast of Nevis, is a hidden gem known for its natural beauty and tranquil ambiance. The pristine beach is lined with coconut palms and offers a serene setting for sunbathing and swimming. Snorkeling and diving enthusiasts can explore the vibrant coral reefs and encounter a variety of tropical fish and marine life. Sandy Bank Bay is a secluded and peaceful retreat where you can escape the hustle and bustle of everyday life.

9. Turtle Beach (St. Kitts):

Turtle Beach, located on the southeastern coast of St. Kitts, is a protected nesting ground for endangered sea turtles. The beach offers a unique opportunity to witness the nesting and hatching of these magnificent creatures. Visitors can participate in guided turtle watching tours and learn about the conservation efforts to protect these endangered species. Turtle Beach also provides a picturesque setting for sunbathing, picnicking, and enjoying the calm waters.

10. Pump Bay (Nevis):

Pump Bay, situated on the northern coast of Nevis, is a secluded and unspoiled beach that offers a peaceful and idyllic retreat. The beach is known for its pristine sands, turquoise waters, and lush green surroundings. Visitors can relax under the shade of palm trees, swim in the calm waters, or explore the vibrant coral reefs through snorkeling or diving. Pump Bay is a hidden gem where you can unwind and connect with nature.

7 Beautiful Plantations and Historic Estates to See

St. Kitts and Nevis are home to several stunning plantations and historic estates that offer a glimpse into the rich history and cultural heritage of the islands. From the beautifully preserved ruins of Wingfield Estate to the serene gardens of Golden Rock Inn, each destination provides a unique experience and a deeper understanding of the islands' past. Whether you're interested in history, architecture, or simply appreciating the natural beauty of the estates, these plantations are a must-visit when exploring St. Kitts and Nevis. So, take your time to explore these fascinating sites and immerse yourself in the captivating stories of the islands' past.

Romney Manor (St. Kitts):

Romney Manor, located in St. Kitts, is a historic plantation that dates back to the 17th century. It is home to the famous Caribelle Batik, a textile studio where artisans create unique hand-painted fabrics. Visitors can explore the lush gardens surrounding the manor, which are filled with vibrant tropical flowers and ancient trees. The estate also offers guided tours that provide insights into the history of the plantation and its significance in the island's past. Entrance to Romney Manor typically costs around $10 USD per person.

Wingfield Estate (St. Kitts):

Wingfield Estate, situated in St. Kitts, is a well-preserved historic site that offers a glimpse into the island's colonial past. The estate features ruins of a sugar mill, a rum distillery, and other structures that showcase the island's once-thriving sugar industry. Visitors can take guided tours of the estate and learn about the process of sugar production and the lives of the enslaved workers. The estate is also home to beautiful gardens and a small museum. Entrance to Wingfield Estate generally costs around $8 USD per person.

New River Estate (Nevis):

New River Estate, located in Nevis, is a historic plantation that provides a fascinating insight into the island's agricultural heritage. The estate offers guided tours that take visitors through the lush gardens and past the remnants of the old sugar mill and other plantation structures. The tour provides a comprehensive understanding of the plantation's history and the processes involved in sugar production. Entrance to New River Estate is typically priced at around $10 USD per person.

Hermitage Plantation (Nevis):

Hermitage Plantation, nestled in the hills of Nevis, is a charming estate that offers a unique blend of history, natural beauty, and warm hospitality. The plantation dates back to the 17th century and features well-preserved plantation buildings, including the Great House, which has been converted into a cozy inn. Visitors can take guided tours of the property, stroll through the beautiful gardens, and enjoy a traditional Nevisian lunch or dinner at the plantation's renowned restaurant. Prices for guided tours and meals at Hermitage Plantation vary depending on the specific offerings.

Golden Rock Inn (Nevis):

Golden Rock Inn, situated in Nevis, is a historic plantation turned boutique hotel and art gallery. The estate boasts lush tropical gardens, stunning ocean views, and a peaceful atmosphere. Visitors can explore the grounds and admire the art installations scattered throughout the property. The plantation also features a restaurant that serves delicious Caribbean-inspired cuisine. While there is no entrance fee to visit Golden Rock Inn, accommodation and dining prices vary depending on the chosen options.

Cottle Church and Estate (St. Kitts):

Cottle Church and Estate, located in St. Kitts, is a significant historical site that showcases the island's cultural and architectural heritage. The estate was once a thriving sugar plantation and is now home to the Cottle Church, which holds the distinction of being the only church in the Caribbean built by slaves. Visitors can explore the church and its surrounding grounds, learning about its history and the role it played in the emancipation movement. There is no entrance fee to visit Cottle Church and Estate, but donations are appreciated.

Montpelier Plantation and Beach (Nevis):

Montpelier Plantation, situated in Nevis, is a luxury hotel that combines the charm of a historic plantation with modern amenities. The estate dates back to the 18th century and offers visitors a chance to explore its beautifully landscaped gardens, enjoy fine dining experiences, and relax by the pool. The property also has access to a private beach, where guests can indulge in water sports activities or simply unwind on the pristine sands. Prices for accommodation and amenities at Montpelier Plantation vary based on the chosen packages and services.

My Top 5 Wonderful Hot Springs and Thermal Baths You Need to See

St. Kitts and Nevis are blessed with a variety of wonderful hot springs and thermal baths that offer unique experiences and therapeutic benefits. Whether you choose to soak in the healing waters of the Bath Hotel and Spring House in Nevis, enjoy a mud bath at the Sulfur Springs in St. Kitts, or create your own hot tub at Hot Springs Bay, each destination provides a rejuvenating and memorable experience. Here's a comprehensive list to my top 5 wonderful hot springs and thermal baths you need to see in St. Kitts and Nevis:

Bath Hotel and Spring House (Nevis):

The Bath Hotel and Spring House in Nevis is a historic site renowned for its natural hot springs. This charming establishment dates back to the late 18th century and offers visitors a unique opportunity to soak in the healing waters of the hot springs.

The Bath Hotel and Spring House provides a range of amenities, including private bathhouses where you can enjoy a relaxing soak in the warm mineral-rich waters. The therapeutic properties of the springs are believed to provide numerous health benefits, including stress relief and improved circulation. The Bath Hotel and Spring House is a must-visit destination for those seeking relaxation and rejuvenation.

Sulfur Springs (St. Kitts):

The Sulfur Springs in St. Kitts are a natural wonder known for their healing properties. These hot springs are located near the Mount Liamuiga volcano and are rich in minerals such as sulfur, calcium, and magnesium. Visitors can experience the therapeutic effects of the springs by taking a dip in the warm waters or indulging in a mud bath.

The mineral-rich mud is said to have detoxifying and rejuvenating properties for the skin. The Sulfur Springs offer a unique and invigorating experience that combines the natural beauty of the surroundings with the healing power of the springs.

Hot Springs Bay (Nevis):

Hot Springs Bay in Nevis is a hidden gem nestled on the western coast of the island. This secluded beach is known for its natural hot spring that emerges from the sand and mixes with the cool ocean waters, creating a delightful thermal experience.

Visitors can dig their own hot tubs in the sand and enjoy a soak in the warm waters while listening to the waves crashing nearby.

The combination of the soothing heat and the picturesque beach setting makes Hot Springs Bay a truly magical place to unwind and relax.

Bloody Point Hot Springs (Nevis):

Bloody Point Hot Springs, located on the southern coast of Nevis, is a captivating natural phenomenon. The hot springs emerge from the volcanic rocks and form small pools along the shoreline. The mineral-rich waters are believed to have healing properties and are particularly beneficial for those with arthritis and other joint-related ailments.

Visitors can take a dip in the warm pools, enjoy the stunning views of the Caribbean Sea, and let the therapeutic waters work their magic. Bloody Point Hot Springs offer a unique and off-the-beaten-path experience for those seeking a natural spa-like retreat.

Belle Mont Farm Hot Pools (St. Kitts):

Belle Mont Farm, a luxurious eco-resort in St. Kitts, is home to a series of private hot pools that offer a secluded and serene experience. Nestled amidst lush tropical gardens, the hot pools provide a tranquil space for guests to unwind and enjoy the therapeutic benefits of the warm waters. Each pool offers a unique ambiance and breathtaking views of the surrounding landscapes.

Visitors can also indulge in spa treatments and wellness therapies inspired by the natural elements found on the island.

The Belle Mont Farm Hot Pools provide a luxurious and rejuvenating retreat for those seeking relaxation and tranquility.

Visiting St. Kitts and Nevis for the best Experience

The Best time of the year to visit St. Kitts and Nevis?

St. Kitts and Nevis, located in the Eastern Caribbean, enjoy a tropical climate with warm temperatures and abundant sunshine throughout the year. When planning a visit to these beautiful islands, it's important to consider the best time to experience favorable weather conditions, vibrant festivals, and fewer crowds. In this chapter, I'll explore the different seasons and highlight the best time of the year to visit St. Kitts and Nevis.

High Season (December to April):

The high season, also known as the peak season, is the most popular time to visit St. Kitts and Nevis. It runs from December to April and coincides with the winter months in North America and Europe. During this time, the islands experience pleasant temperatures ranging from the mid-70s to mid-80s Fahrenheit (mid-20s to low 30s Celsius). The weather is generally dry, with minimal rainfall and lower humidity levels. Visitors can expect clear skies, calm seas, and perfect beach weather.

The high season is also the time when the islands host several exciting festivals and events. The St. Kitts Music Festival, held in June, features internationally renowned artists, while the Nevis Mango and Food Festival, held in July, celebrates the island's delicious mangoes and culinary delights.

These festivals showcase the vibrant culture, music, and cuisine of the islands, providing visitors with a memorable experience.

Shoulder Season (May to June and November):

The shoulder seasons, which include May to June and November, are transitional periods between the high and low seasons. These months offer a great balance of favorable weather, fewer crowds, and potential cost savings. The temperatures remain warm, with daytime highs in the 80s Fahrenheit (around 30 degrees Celsius), making it ideal for outdoor activities and beach relaxation.

While there may be occasional showers during the shoulder seasons, rainfall is generally brief and doesn't significantly impact travel plans. It's worth noting that May and June are considered the start of the rainy season, so it's advisable to pack a light rain jacket or umbrella. Additionally, November marks the end of the hurricane season, reducing the chances of encountering any severe weather disturbances.

Low Season (July to October):

The low season, from July to October, is characterized by higher temperatures, increased humidity, and a higher chance of rainfall. These months coincide with the Caribbean hurricane season, which officially runs from June to November. While the risk of encountering a hurricane is relatively low, it's important to monitor weather forecasts and purchase travel insurance that covers unforeseen weather events.

Despite the higher temperatures and occasional showers, the low season offers several advantages. The islands are less crowded, and accommodations, flights, and tours may offer discounted rates and special promotions.

Additionally, the lush vegetation and vibrant flowers create a picturesque backdrop, and wildlife enthusiasts can witness sea turtles nesting on the beaches.

Festivals and Events:

St. Kitts and Nevis are known for their vibrant festivals and cultural events, which take place throughout the year. The Carnival celebrations, held in St. Kitts in December and Nevis in January, are the highlight of the cultural calendar. These lively festivities feature colorful parades, calypso music, traditional dances, and vibrant costumes, providing a true taste of Caribbean culture.

Other notable events include the St. Kitts Music Festival in June, the Nevis Mango and Food Festival in July, and the Culturama Festival in Nevis, which spans two weeks in July and August.

These festivals showcase the islands' rich heritage, music, cuisine, and traditions, offering visitors an immersive cultural experience.

When to Avoid visiting St. Kitts and Nevis?

St. Kitts and Nevis, the stunning twin islands in the Caribbean, are popular destinations known for their pristine beaches, lush landscapes, and vibrant culture. While these islands offer a year-round tropical paradise, there are certain periods when it's advisable to avoid visiting due to potential weather-related challenges and other considerations. In this section, I'll explore when it's best to avoid visiting St. Kitts and Nevis to ensure a smooth and enjoyable trip.

Hurricane Season (June to November):

One of the primary factors to consider when planning a visit to St. Kitts and Nevis is the Caribbean hurricane season, which officially runs from June to November. During this period, the islands are more susceptible to tropical storms and hurricanes. While the islands have measures in place to handle such events, it's advisable to avoid visiting during this time to minimize the risk of encountering severe weather conditions.

Hurricanes and tropical storms can disrupt travel plans, close businesses, and even cause damage to infrastructure. It's essential to monitor weather forecasts and heed any warnings issued by local authorities. If you do choose to visit during the hurricane season, consider purchasing travel insurance that covers unforeseen weather events and provides flexibility for rescheduling or canceling your trip.

Rainy Season (May to November):

The rainy season in St. Kitts and Nevis typically spans from May to November. While rain showers can occur throughout the year, this period experiences higher rainfall and increased humidity. The rainy season is characterized by brief but intense showers, often followed by clear skies. These showers can provide relief from the heat and add to the lush greenery of the islands, but they can also impact outdoor activities and beach visits.

If you prefer consistent sunshine and dry weather, it's best to avoid visiting during the rainy season. However, it's worth noting that the islands' landscapes are at their most vibrant during this time, with blooming flowers and lush vegetation. Additionally, accommodations and activities may offer discounted rates during the rainy season, making it an attractive option for budget-conscious travelers.

Peak Cruise Ship Days:

St. Kitts and Nevis are popular cruise ship destinations, with numerous ships docking at the islands' ports throughout the year. On peak cruise ship days, the islands can experience an influx of tourists, resulting in crowded attractions, beaches, and restaurants. If you prefer a more relaxed and tranquil experience, it's advisable to check the cruise ship schedules and plan your visit on days when fewer ships are in port.

By avoiding peak cruise ship days, you can have a more authentic experience of the islands, explore attractions at your own pace, and enjoy the beaches without the crowds. Keep in mind that cruise ship schedules can change, so it's essential to check the latest information before finalizing your travel plans.

Major Holidays and Events:

During major holidays and local events, St. Kitts and Nevis can become busier, and accommodations may be in high demand. It's important to consider the impact of these events on your travel experience. The Carnival celebrations, for example, attract large crowds and can lead to increased prices for flights and accommodations. If you prefer a quieter visit, it's advisable to avoid these peak periods and opt for a different time when the islands are less crowded.

Some major events and holidays to be aware of include Christmas and New Year's, Carnival celebrations (held in December and January), and the St. Kitts Music Festival (held in June). These events can provide a lively and exciting atmosphere, but they may also result in higher prices and limited availability.

How to Stay Safe in St. Kitts and Nevis?

St. Kitts and Nevis, the enchanting twin islands in the Caribbean, are known for their natural beauty, warm hospitality, and vibrant culture. While these islands offer a safe and welcoming environment for visitors, it's important to take necessary precautions to ensure a secure and enjoyable stay. In this section, I will discussing the essential tips and guidelines to help you stay safe in St. Kitts and Nevis.

Research and Plan Ahead:

Before traveling to St. Kitts and Nevis, it's essential to conduct thorough research and plan your trip accordingly. Familiarize yourself with the local customs, traditions, and laws of the islands. Take note of any travel advisories or warnings issued by your country's government or international organizations. Stay informed about the local weather conditions, including hurricane alerts during the hurricane season, and adjust your plans accordingly.

Choose Safe Accommodations:

When selecting accommodations in St. Kitts and Nevis, prioritize reputable and well-established establishments. Consider factors such as location, security measures, and guest reviews. Opt for accommodations that have 24-hour front desk services, secure entrances, and well-lit common areas. If you're renting a vacation home or villa, ensure that it's from a trusted source and located in a safe neighborhood.

Practice Personal Safety Precautions:

Maintaining personal safety precautions is crucial in any destination, and St. Kitts and Nevis are no exception. Here are some important tips to follow:

a. **Be aware of your surroundings**: Stay vigilant and aware of your surroundings, especially in crowded tourist areas or unfamiliar neighborhoods. Avoid displaying valuable items, such as expensive jewelry or large amounts of cash, which can attract unwanted attention.

b. **Use secure transportation:** Choose licensed taxis or reputable transportation services to ensure your safety during your journeys. If you're renting a vehicle, familiarize yourself with local driving laws, road conditions, and safety guidelines.

c. **Keep important documents secure:** Safeguard your travel documents, including your passport, identification, and travel insurance. It's recommended to keep electronic copies of these documents in a secure cloud storage service as a backup.

d. **Avoid walking alone at night**: While St. Kitts and Nevis are generally safe, it's advisable to avoid walking alone at night, especially in poorly lit or isolated areas. If you need to venture out after dark, consider using reputable transportation options or travel in a group.

Respect the Local Culture:

Respecting the local culture and customs is essential for a harmonious and safe experience in St. Kitts and Nevis.

Dress modestly when visiting religious sites or local communities. Observe and follow any specific guidelines or restrictions at cultural or religious events. Engage with locals respectfully and be mindful of cultural sensitivities.

Practice Water Safety:

St. Kitts and Nevis offer stunning beaches and opportunities for water activities, but it's important to prioritize water safety. Follow these guidelines:

a. **Swim in designated areas**: Stick to beaches with lifeguards and swim within designated areas. Pay attention to warning flags or signs indicating dangerous conditions.

b. **Be cautious of strong currents**: Some beaches may have strong currents or undertows. Familiarize yourself with the beach conditions and exercise caution when swimming.

c. **Use appropriate safety equipment**: If you're engaging in water sports such as snorkeling, diving, or boating, ensure you have the necessary safety equipment and follow the instructions of trained professionals.

Health and Medical Considerations:

Prioritize your health and well-being during your visit to St. Kitts and Nevis:

a. **Obtain travel insurance**: It's recommended to have comprehensive travel insurance that covers medical emergencies, trip cancellation, and other unforeseen circumstances.

b. **Stay hydrated**: The Caribbean climate can be hot and humid. Drink plenty of water to stay hydrated, especially when engaging in outdoor activities.

c. **Take precautions against mosquito-borne illnesses**: St. Kitts and Nevis have a tropical climate, and mosquitoes can be present. Protect yourself by using insect repellent, wearing long sleeves and pants, and staying in accommodations with screens or air conditioning.

d. **Seek medical advice and vaccinations**: Consult with your healthcare provider before traveling to St. Kitts and Nevis to ensure you are up to date on necessary vaccinations and receive any recommended medications or preventive measures.

Emergency Contacts and Communication:

Before your trip, make note of important emergency contacts, including the local police, hospital, and your country's embassy or consulate in St. Kitts and Nevis. Ensure that you have a reliable means of communication, such as a working mobile phone with local and emergency numbers saved.

Is St. Kitts and Nevis Safe for International Students?

St. Kitts and Nevis, the picturesque twin islands in the Caribbean, are not only popular tourist destinations but also emerging educational hubs. With their stunning landscapes, vibrant culture, and welcoming community, these islands have attracted an increasing number of international students. If you are considering pursuing your education in St. Kitts and Nevis, you may wonder about the safety and security of these islands. In this chapter, I will explore the safety aspects of St. Kitts and Nevis for international students.

Low Crime Rate:

St. Kitts and Nevis have a relatively low crime rate compared to many other Caribbean countries. The islands have made significant efforts to ensure the safety of residents and visitors. The local police force is present and active, working to maintain law and order. While petty theft and opportunistic crimes can occur, violent crimes are rare, and instances of serious crime are isolated.

Safe Campuses and Educational Institutions:

The universities and colleges in St. Kitts and Nevis prioritize the safety and well-being of their students. Many educational institutions have campus security measures in place, including surveillance systems, access control, and security personnel. Campus environments are generally considered safe, and students can feel secure while attending classes and participating in campus activities.

Welcoming and Supportive Community:

The people of St. Kitts and Nevis are known for their warm hospitality and friendly nature. The local community embraces international students, creating an inclusive and supportive environment. Students often find it easy to integrate into the community and develop lasting relationships. The sense of community helps foster a sense of safety and well-being among international students.

Student Housing Options:

Many educational institutions in St. Kitts and Nevis offer on-campus or off-campus student housing options. These accommodations are designed with student safety in mind, providing secure access, well-lit common areas, and staff who can address any concerns. When choosing off-campus housing, it's important to select reputable landlords and ensure that the accommodation meets your safety requirements.

Safety Precautions for International Students:

To enhance personal safety, it is advisable for international students to take certain precautions:

a. **Stay informed:** Keep yourself updated about any safety advisories or guidelines issued by your educational institution or local authorities. Stay aware of your surroundings and be mindful of any changes in the safety situation.

b. **Secure your belongings**: Avoid carrying large amounts of cash or valuable items with you. Use lockers or secure storage options for your personal belongings. It's also recommended to have travel insurance that covers your possessions in case of loss or theft.

c. **Maintain communication:** Provide emergency contact information to your educational institution and keep your mobile phone charged and with you at all times. Familiarize yourself with local emergency numbers and know how to contact the local police or campus security in case of an emergency.

d. **Travel in groups:** When exploring the islands or participating in off-campus activities, it's safer to travel in groups or pairs, especially during nighttime.

Health and Well-being:

St. Kitts and Nevis have reputable medical facilities and healthcare services to cater to the needs of international students. It's important to maintain good health by following basic hygiene practices, staying hydrated, and seeking medical attention when necessary. International students are encouraged to obtain health insurance that covers medical expenses and emergency medical evacuation if required.

Cultural Sensitivity:

Respecting the local culture and customs is crucial for international students. Familiarize yourself with the local traditions, norms, and laws to ensure a harmonious experience. Dress modestly when appropriate and be mindful of local sensitivities. Developing an understanding and appreciation for the local culture will contribute to a positive and safe experience in St. Kitts and Nevis.

Packing Essentials for Your trip

When planning a trip to St. Kitts and Nevis, it is essential to pack wisely to ensure a comfortable and enjoyable experience. These stunning Caribbean islands offer a mix of beautiful beaches, outdoor adventures, and cultural attractions. To help you make the most of your trip, I have compiled a detailed list of packing essentials that will ensure you are well-prepared for your adventure in St. Kitts and Nevis.

Clothing:

St. Kitts and Nevis enjoy a warm tropical climate year-round, so pack lightweight and breathable clothing. Here's what you should consider:

- **Swimwear**: Don't forget to pack your swimsuit for enjoying the pristine beaches.
- **Light, loose-fitting clothing**: Opt for comfortable clothes such as shorts, t-shirts, and sundresses.
- **Sun protection:** Sunscreen, wide-brimmed hats, and sunglasses are crucial to protect yourself from the sun's strong rays.

- **Rain gear**: Pack a lightweight rain jacket or poncho as the islands may experience occasional showers.

Footwear:

Choose footwear that is comfortable and suitable for various activities:

- **Sandals or flip-flops:** Ideal for beach outings and casual walks.
- **Walking or hiking shoes:** If you plan on exploring the islands' nature trails or engaging in outdoor activities, sturdy shoes are recommended.

Electronics:

While you may want to disconnect and enjoy the natural beauty of St. Kitts and Nevis, some electronics are essential:

- **Travel adapter:** The islands use 230V electrical outlets, so bring a universal adapter to charge your devices.
- **Camera or smartphone**: Capture the breathtaking landscapes and vibrant culture of the islands.

Travel Documents:

To ensure a smooth trip, don't forget to pack the following important documents:

- **Passport:** Ensure it is valid for at least six months beyond your intended stay.
- **Visa (if required):** Check the entry requirements beforehand to determine if you need a visa.

Printed copies of travel itineraries, hotel reservations, and any other relevant documents.

Health and Safety:

Pack the following items to ensure your health and safety during your trip:

- **Prescription medications:** Bring an ample supply for the duration of your stay.
- **Basic first aid kit**: Include band-aids, antiseptic ointment, pain relievers, and any personal medication.
- **Insect repellent:** Protect yourself from mosquitoes, especially during dusk and dawn.
- **Travel insurance**: Consider purchasing comprehensive travel insurance to cover any unforeseen events.

Beach and Outdoor Essentials:

As you'll likely spend a significant amount of time enjoying the beaches and outdoor activities, remember to pack these essentials:

- **Beach towel**: Opt for a lightweight and quick-drying towel for beach outings.
- **Snorkeling gear:** If you have your own snorkeling equipment, bring it along to explore the vibrant marine life.
- **Day backpack**: A small backpack will come in handy for carrying essentials during hikes or day trips.
- **Reusable water bottle**: Stay hydrated by carrying a refillable water bottle.

Money and Miscellaneous:

Don't forget these miscellaneous items that can enhance your trip:

- **Sufficient cash:** While credit cards are widely accepted, it's a good idea to have some cash for smaller establishments and emergencies.
- **Travel lock**: Secure your luggage and hotel room with a reliable travel lock.

Travel guidebook or maps: Consider bringing a guidebook or printed maps to explore the islands and discover hidden gems.

Contact Information for Embassies and Consulates

When traveling abroad, it is essential to have access to the contact information of your country's embassy or consulate. Embassies and consulates serve as vital resources, providing assistance and support to citizens in a foreign country. In this chapter, I will provide you with important contact information for embassies and consulates, ensuring that you are well-prepared and have access to the necessary assistance during your travels.

Understanding the Role of Embassies and Consulates:

- **Embassies**: Embassies represent the sending country in the host country and handle diplomatic relations.
- **Consulates**: Consulates provide various consular services, including assisting citizens, issuing visas, and promoting trade and cultural relations.

Locating Your Country's Embassy or Consulate:

- **Government Websites:** Visit your government's official website and navigate to the section on foreign affairs or consular services.
- **Online Directories:** Use online directories that list embassies and consulates worldwide, such as the embassy/consulate finder tools provided by government websites or specialized directories like embassypages.com.

Contact Information for Embassies and Consulates:

- **Embassy/Consulate Address:** Obtain the physical address of the embassy or consulate in your destination country.
- **Telephone Numbers**: Note down the general contact number for the embassy or consulate. It may also include emergency contact numbers.
- **Email Address**: Obtain the official email address for non-emergency communication.
- **Fax Number:** Some embassies and consulates still use fax machines, so it's helpful to have their fax number as well.

Social Media: Many embassies and consulates maintain social media accounts where you can find updates, news, and contact information.

Emergency Assistance:

- **Emergency Hotline**: Check if your embassy or consulate has a dedicated emergency hotline for urgent situations.
- **24/7 Contact**: Determine if there is a 24/7 emergency contact number or an after-hours duty officer available.

Registration and Travel Alerts:

- **Registration**: Some embassies and consulates provide an online registration system for citizens traveling or residing abroad. Consider registering your trip to receive important updates and safety information.
- **Travel Alerts and Warnings:** Stay informed about travel advisories, alerts, and warnings issued by your embassy or consulate. These provide crucial information regarding safety concerns, political instability, natural disasters, or other significant events.

Consular Services:

- **Passport Services:** Embassies and consulates can assist with passport-related matters, including renewals, replacements, and issuing emergency travel documents.
- **Visa Services:** If you require a visa to enter your destination country, the embassy or consulate can provide guidance and process your visa application.
- **Notarial Services:** Embassies and consulates may offer notarial services, such as certifying documents, administering oaths, or witnessing signatures.
- **Legal and Financial Assistance:** In case of legal issues or financial emergencies, embassies and consulates can provide guidance and connect you with local resources.
- **Lost or Stolen Belongings**: If you lose your passport or other important documents, contact your embassy or consulate for assistance and guidance.

Cultural and Community Services:

- **Events and Celebrations:** Embassies and consulates often organize cultural events, celebrations, or exhibitions to promote their country's culture and foster community connections.

- **Educational and Exchange Programs**: They may offer educational and exchange programs, scholarships, or resources for studying abroad.
- **Consular Outreach**: Some embassies and consulates conduct outreach programs to support the local community, provide consular services, or address specific needs of their citizens abroad.

This page was left blank intentionally

Outdoors Experience in St Kitts and Nevis:

When is the best time to Scuba Diving and Snorkeling?

Choosing the best time for scuba diving and snorkeling is crucial to ensure optimal conditions, breathtaking marine life encounters, and an unforgettable underwater experience. Consider factors such as weather patterns, water visibility, water temperature, marine life activity, crowd levels, local regulations, and dive conditions. Scuba diving and snorkeling offer captivating underwater adventures, allowing enthusiasts to discover the mesmerizing beauty of marine life.

However, choosing the right time to embark on these activities can significantly enhance the experience. In this chapter, I will provide you with the best times for scuba diving and snorkeling, taking into account factors such as weather conditions, water visibility, marine life encounters, and crowd levels.

Weather and Seasons:

- **Dry Season**: Many diving destinations have a dry season characterized by minimal rainfall, making it an ideal time for underwater exploration. Check the weather patterns of your desired location to determine the dry season.
- **Stormy Season**: Avoid diving during stormy seasons or periods with high chances of hurricanes or tropical storms, as these conditions can compromise safety and visibility.

Water Visibility:

- **Clear Water Conditions**: Optimal diving and snorkeling experiences occur when water visibility is at its best. This is typically influenced by factors such as calm seas, minimal rainfall, and low sedimentation.
- **Algae Blooms:** Avoid visiting destinations during periods of excessive algae blooms, as they can reduce visibility and hinder marine life sightings.

Water Temperature:

- **Optimal Temperatures:** Consider the water temperature that suits your preferences. Some divers prefer warmer waters, while others enjoy colder temperatures. Research the average water temperatures of your desired location during different times of the year.

Marine Life Activity:

- **Mating and Migration Seasons**: Many underwater creatures have specific mating and migration seasons. Research the local marine life of your diving destination to plan your trip during periods when you are likely to encounter vibrant displays of marine activity.
- **Whale Shark and Manta Ray Encounters:** Certain diving destinations are known for seasonal visits from majestic creatures like whale sharks and manta rays. Plan your trip accordingly to maximize your chances of encountering these incredible species.

Avoiding Crowds:

- **High Season**: Popular diving spots may experience high tourist seasons when beaches and dive sites are crowded. Consider visiting during shoulder seasons or less busy periods to enjoy a more tranquil experience and have better access to dive sites.

- **Weekdays vs. Weekends**: Opt for diving and snorkeling excursions on weekdays, as weekends tend to be busier due to local and international visitors.

Local Regulations and Dive Conditions:

- **Restricted Seasons:** Some dive sites have specific restrictions or closures during certain times of the year. Research local regulations and dive conditions to ensure your chosen destination is open and accessible during your planned visit.
- **Dive Site Accessibility**: Inquire about the accessibility of specific dive sites during different times of the year. Some sites may be more challenging to access or may require advanced diving skills during certain seasons.

Local Events and Festivals:

- **Dive Festivals:** Some diving destinations host annual dive festivals, offering unique opportunities to explore the underwater world while participating in festivities and special activities. Check the event calendar of your desired location to align your trip with these exciting occasions.

When is the best time to Sailing and Yachting?

Sailing and yachting offer an exhilarating way to explore the open waters and embrace the freedom of the sea. To make the most of your sailing or yachting adventure, it is essential to choose the right time that aligns with optimal weather conditions, wind patterns, sea states, and other factors. In this section, I will delve into the best time for sailing and yachting, taking into account various considerations that can enhance your experience on the water.

Weather Conditions:

- **Mild Temperatures:** Consider sailing during seasons with mild temperatures, providing comfortable conditions for your journey. Extreme heat or cold may affect your comfort and enjoyment.
- **Avoid Stormy Seasons**: Steer clear of stormy seasons or regions prone to hurricanes and cyclones. These conditions can pose risks to safety and result in challenging sailing conditions.

Wind Patterns:

- **Optimal Wind Speed:** Seek sailing opportunities during periods when wind conditions are favorable. Moderate and consistent winds allow for smoother sailing experiences, enabling you to enjoy the thrill of cruising through the water.
- **Local Wind Effects:** Research the local wind effects of your chosen sailing destination. Certain regions may experience unique wind patterns influenced by geographical features, such as local land and sea breezes or thermal winds.

Sea States:

- **Calm Seas:** Plan your sailing or yachting adventure during times when the sea is generally calm, minimizing the chances of encountering rough or choppy waters. Smooth sailing conditions ensure a more enjoyable and comfortable experience on board.
- **Swell and Wave Heights**: Keep an eye on swell and wave forecasts to gauge the expected sea conditions. Excessive swells or high wave heights may result in uncomfortable or unsafe sailing conditions.

Daylight Hours:

Longer Days: Longer daylight hours provide additional time for sailing and enjoying the scenic beauty of your surroundings. Consider the time of year when daylight hours are at their peak, allowing for extended sailing expeditions and memorable sunsets on the water.

Off-Season Advantages:

- **Fewer Crowds**: Sailing during the off-season or shoulder seasons often means encountering fewer crowds and enjoying more secluded anchorages and marinas. This provides a quieter and more tranquil sailing experience.
- **Potential Discounts:** Off-season periods may offer cost savings, as charter companies and marinas often provide discounted rates. Research the pricing options and availability during different times of the year.

Special Events and Regattas:

- **Sailing Events:** Check if there are any renowned sailing events or regattas happening in your desired destination. Participating or witnessing these events can add excitement and a sense of camaraderie to your sailing experience.

- **Cultural Festivals:** Explore if there are any cultural festivals or celebrations taking place in coastal areas. Combining sailing with local festivities can provide a unique and enriching experience.

Local Knowledge and Expertise:

- **Consult Local Sailors:** Tap into the knowledge of local sailors, yacht clubs, or sailing communities in the area you plan to visit. They can offer valuable insights into the best times for sailing, preferred routes, and insider tips.
- **Sailing Guides and Resources:** Utilize sailing guides, cruising handbooks, and online resources that provide information on optimal sailing seasons, navigational tips, and local conditions.

When is the best time to go Deep Sea Fishing?

Deep sea fishing is a thrilling adventure that allows anglers to test their skills and reel in impressive catches from the depths of the ocean. To optimize your chances of a successful and memorable fishing trip, it's crucial to choose the right time that aligns with favorable conditions for fish activity, weather patterns, and other factors. In this detailed section, I will explore the best time for deep sea fishing, considering various aspects that can enhance your experience on the open waters.

Fish Availability and Seasonality:

- **Research Targeted Species:** Identify the target species you wish to catch and learn about their migration patterns, spawning seasons, and preferred feeding grounds. This knowledge will help you determine the best time to encounter specific fish species.
- **Local Regulations**: Familiarize yourself with local fishing regulations and restrictions to ensure you are fishing during legal and sustainable seasons for your desired species.

Weather Conditions:

- **Stable Weather**: Opt for periods of stable weather conditions with calm seas and minimal chances of storms or strong winds. Stable weather provides a safer and more enjoyable fishing experience.
- **Temperature Considerations**: Fish behavior can be influenced by water temperature. Research the preferred temperature ranges for your targeted species and plan your trip accordingly.

Water Conditions:

- **Currents and Upwellings:** Study the ocean currents and upwellings in the area you plan to fish. These can impact the movement and concentration of fish, as well as affect baitfish activity, which, in turn, attracts larger predators.
- **Water Clarity:** Clear water conditions are generally favorable for deep sea fishing as they enhance visibility and increase the likelihood of spotting fish.

Time of Day:

- **Early Morning and Late Afternoon:** Fishing during the early morning and late afternoon often yields better results, as fish are more active during these periods.

Take advantage of the feeding patterns of your targeted species to increase your chances of success.

Lunar Phase:

- **Full Moon and New Moon:** Some anglers believe that fishing during the full moon or new moon phases can increase fish activity. These lunar phases can influence tide levels, which, in turn, affect the availability of prey and the feeding behavior of fish.

Local Knowledge and Expertise:

- **Consult Local Fishermen:** Reach out to local fishermen or fishing charters with experience in the area you plan to fish. They can provide valuable insights into the best times, techniques, and locations for deep sea fishing.
- **Fishing Reports and Forums:** Stay updated with fishing reports and online forums dedicated to the region you wish to explore. These platforms often share real-time information on recent catches, hotspots, and recommended fishing times.

Consider the Off-Season:

Lower Fishing Pressure: Fishing during the off-season or shoulder seasons can provide benefits, such as reduced competition from other anglers and less fishing pressure on the targeted species.

Potential Discounts: Charter companies or fishing lodges may offer discounted rates during the off-season, making it an economical choice for avid anglers.

When is the best time to go Golfing and Tennis?

Golfing and tennis are two popular outdoor sports that offer enjoyment, exercise, and opportunities for friendly competition. To make the most of your golfing or tennis experience, it is essential to choose the right time that aligns with favorable weather conditions, crowd levels, course or court availability, and other factors. In this section, I will delve into the best time for golfing and tennis, considering various aspects that can enhance your sporting endeavors.

Golfing:

a) **Weather Conditions:**

Mild Temperatures: Opt for seasons with mild temperatures, which provide comfortable playing conditions. Extreme heat or cold may affect your performance and enjoyment.

Dry Weather: Choose periods with lower chances of rainfall to avoid interruptions and enjoy a smoother game.

b) **Course Conditions:**

Course Maintenance: Consider the course maintenance schedule. Courses typically undergo maintenance during certain times of the year, which may impact playing conditions.

Busy Seasons: Avoid peak seasons when golf courses are crowded with players, as this can result in slower play and reduced availability of tee times.

c) **Local Events and Tournaments:**

Golfing Events: Check if there are any major golf events or tournaments happening in the area you plan to visit. Witnessing professional tournaments can add excitement and inspiration to your golfing experience.

Tennis:

a) **Weather Conditions:**

Moderate Temperatures: Look for seasons with moderate temperatures that allow for comfortable gameplay. Extreme heat or cold may affect your performance and increase the risk of injuries.

Dry Weather: Choose periods with lower chances of rainfall to minimize court closures and ensure uninterrupted gameplay.

b) **Court Availability:**

Peak Hours: Avoid peak hours when courts are in high demand. Consider booking your court time during less busy periods to enjoy longer playing sessions.

Club Memberships: If you plan to play at a tennis club, inquire about membership benefits, which may include priority court bookings and access to exclusive facilities.

c) **Local Tournaments and Leagues:**

Tennis Events: Check if there are any local tennis tournaments or leagues taking place during your visit. Participating or watching these events can add excitement and a sense of community to your tennis experience.

Crowd Levels:

Weekdays vs. Weekends: Opt for playing golf or tennis on weekdays, as weekends tend to be busier due to local players and visitors. This allows for a more relaxed and enjoyable experience with less waiting time.

Off-peak Hours: Consider playing during off-peak hours, such as early mornings or late afternoons, to avoid crowded courses or courts.

Personal Preferences:

Comfortable Playing Conditions: Consider your personal preference for weather conditions and playing environment. Some players may enjoy the challenge of playing in windier or hotter conditions, while others prefer milder climates.

Skill Level: Take into account your skill level and experience. If you are a beginner, playing during less crowded times may provide a more relaxed atmosphere to focus on improving your game.

Local Knowledge and Expertise:

Consult Local Players: Reach out to local golfers or tennis enthusiasts for insights into the best times to play, recommended courses or clubs, and local tips for an enjoyable experience.

Online Resources: Utilize online resources, forums, and social media groups dedicated to golfing and tennis. These platforms often share valuable information on local playing conditions, course reviews, and recommendations.

When is the best time to go Zip-lining and Canopy Tours?

Zip-lining and canopy tours offer thrilling adventures that allow you to explore the natural beauty of forests and landscapes from a unique perspective. To maximize your zip-lining and canopy tour experience, it's crucial to choose the right time that aligns with optimal weather conditions, wildlife activity, safety considerations, and other factors. In this section, I will delve into the best time for zip-lining and canopy tours, considering various aspects that can enhance your aerial adventure.

Weather Conditions:

a) **Moderate Temperatures**: Opt for seasons with moderate temperatures, as extreme heat or cold can impact your comfort and overall enjoyment during the tour.

b) **Dry Season**: Choose periods with lower chances of rainfall to minimize the risk of tour cancellations or interruptions. Dry weather ensures safer conditions for zip-lining and canopy tours.

Wildlife Activity:

- **Breeding and Mating Seasons:** Research the local wildlife in the area where you plan to go zip-lining and canopy touring. Some regions may have specific seasons when animals are more active, providing opportunities for wildlife sightings and a unique experience.
- **Bird Migration:** Explore if the area is a migratory route for birds. Zip-lining during bird migration seasons can offer a chance to witness diverse bird species in flight.

Foliage and Scenic Views:

- **Foliage Seasons:** Consider the foliage seasons in the area. Spring and fall may present stunning displays of colorful foliage, enhancing the scenic beauty and making your zip-lining and canopy tour even more captivating.
- **Sight Lines**: Choose periods when the foliage is less dense, allowing for better sight lines and unobstructed views of the surrounding landscape.

Safety Considerations:

- **Wind Conditions:** Wind can significantly impact the safety and enjoyment of zip-lining and canopy tours. Opt for days with mild winds, as strong gusts can make the activity challenging or even unsafe.
- **Lightning and Storms:** Avoid zip-lining and canopy tours during stormy or lightning-prone weather conditions. Thunderstorms pose a significant risk, and most tour operators will suspend activities for safety reasons.
- **Tour Operator Recommendations**: Follow the guidance of experienced tour operators who are well-versed in local weather patterns and safety protocols. They can provide insights into the best time to embark on your aerial adventure.

Crowd Levels:

- **Weekdays vs. Weekends:** Consider going on zip-lining and canopy tours during weekdays, as weekends tend to be busier with more visitors. Weekday tours provide a more serene and intimate experience.
- **Off-peak Hours:** Opt for early morning or late afternoon tours to avoid peak hours when crowds are typically larger. This allows for a more relaxed and immersive experience as you glide through the treetops.

Personal Preferences:

- **Comfortable Temperatures**: Take into account your personal preference for weather conditions. Some individuals may enjoy zip-lining and canopy tours in warmer temperatures, while others may prefer cooler climates.
- **Adrenaline Level**: Consider your desired adrenaline level. If you prefer a more adrenaline-pumping experience, choose periods when tour operators offer specialized tours with added challenges or unique features.

Local Knowledge and Expertise:

- **Consult Local Tour Operators:** Seek advice from local tour operators who specialize in zip-lining and canopy tours. They possess valuable insights into the best times to visit, safety considerations, and recommended routes.
- **Online Resources**: Utilize online resources such as travel forums, review websites, and social media groups dedicated to adventure tourism. These platforms often provide firsthand accounts, tips, and recommendations for zip-lining and canopy tours in various locations.

When is the best time to go ATV and Off-Road Adventures?

ATV (All-Terrain Vehicle) and off-road adventures offer an exhilarating way to explore rugged terrains and embrace the thrill of off-road driving. To ensure a memorable and safe experience, it's essential to choose the right time that aligns with favorable weather conditions, trail accessibility, wildlife activity, and other factors. In this chapter, I will delve into the best time for ATV and off-road adventures, considering various aspects that can enhance your adrenaline-fueled journey.

Weather Conditions:

a) **Moderate Temperatures**: Opt for seasons with moderate temperatures, as extreme heat or cold can affect your comfort and overall enjoyment during the adventure.

b) **Dry Season**: Choose periods with lower chances of rainfall to minimize the risk of encountering muddy or impassable trails. Dry weather ensures better traction and safer off-road conditions.

Trail Accessibility:

- **Seasonal Closures:** Research if the trails you plan to explore have any seasonal closures. Some trails may be inaccessible during certain times due to weather conditions, maintenance, or wildlife conservation efforts. Ensure that your chosen trails are open and accessible during your visit.
- **Snow or Ice:** Be aware of areas where snow or ice may affect trail conditions. If you're planning an ATV or off-road adventure in mountainous regions, consider avoiding the winter months when snowfall is prevalent.

Wildlife Activity:

- **Breeding and Mating Seasons:** Familiarize yourself with the breeding and mating seasons of local wildlife in the area where you plan to go on your ATV or off-road adventure. Some seasons may offer opportunities for wildlife sightings and encounters, adding a unique element to your experience.
- **Protected Areas:** Check if the trails pass through protected areas or national parks known for their wildlife populations. These areas may have specific regulations or restrictions during certain times to ensure the safety and conservation of wildlife.

Safety Considerations:

- **Extreme Weather:** Avoid ATV and off-road adventures during severe weather conditions, such as heavy rain, thunderstorms, or high winds. These conditions can make the trails hazardous and compromise your safety.
- **Daylight Hours:** Plan your adventure during daylight hours to ensure better visibility on the trails and reduce the risk of getting lost or encountering unexpected obstacles.
- **Safety Equipment**: Always wear appropriate safety gear, including helmets, goggles, gloves, and sturdy footwear. Adhere to all safety guidelines and instructions provided by tour operators or rental agencies.

Crowd Levels:

- **Weekdays vs. Weekends**: Consider going on ATV and off-road adventures on weekdays to avoid the typically higher crowd levels found on weekends. Weekday adventures provide a more secluded and immersive experience.
- **Off-peak Hours:** Opt for early morning or late afternoon adventures to avoid peak hours when more

visitors are likely to be on the trails. This allows for a more uninterrupted and enjoyable ride.

Personal Preferences:

- **Terrain Preferences:** Consider your preferred terrain for ATV and off-road adventures. Some individuals may enjoy rocky terrains, while others may prefer sandy or forested trails. Research the area you plan to visit to ensure it aligns with your preferences.
- **Adrenaline Level:** Determine your desired level of adrenaline. If you prefer a more challenging and intense experience, consider choosing trails with rugged terrain or additional obstacles.

Local Knowledge and Expertise:

- **Consult Local Guides:** Seek advice from local ATV tour operators or off-road enthusiasts who have experience in the area you plan to visit. They can provide valuable insights into the best times to go, recommended trails, and safety considerations.
- **Online Resources:** Utilize online resources such as ATV forums, travel websites, and social media groups dedicated to off-road adventures. These platforms often

offer firsthand accounts, trail recommendations, and tips for ATV and off-road enthusiasts.

When is the best time to go Horseback Riding and Equestrian Activities?

Horseback riding and equestrian activities offer a unique way to connect with nature, experience the bond between humans and horses, and explore picturesque landscapes. To make the most of your equestrian adventure, it is essential to choose the right time that aligns with favorable weather conditions, trail availability, and other factors. In this chapter, I will delve into the best time for horseback riding and equestrian activities, considering various aspects that can enhance your equine experience.

Weather Conditions:

a) **Moderate Temperatures**: Opt for seasons with moderate temperatures, as extreme heat or cold can affect your comfort and the well-being of the horses. Mild temperatures ensure a pleasant riding experience for both riders and equines.

b) **Dry Season:** Choose periods with lower chances of rainfall to avoid muddy trails, which can make horseback riding challenging and potentially unsafe.

Scenic Beauty:

- **Foliage Seasons**: Consider the foliage seasons in the region where you plan to go horseback riding. Spring and fall often offer stunning displays of colorful foliage, adding a touch of natural beauty to your equestrian experience.
- **Blossoming Periods**: Research if there are specific seasons when wildflowers or other plants bloom in the area. Riding through landscapes adorned with vibrant blooms can create a magical and picturesque ambiance.

Trail Availability:

- **Seasonal Access:** Determine if the trails you wish to explore are accessible year-round or have seasonal closures. Some trails may close during certain times due to weather conditions or to protect wildlife habitats. Ensure that your chosen trails are open and suitable for horseback riding during your visit.
- **Terrain Suitability:** Consider the terrain of the trails. Some trails may be more challenging or suitable for experienced riders, while others are more beginner-

friendly. Choose trails that align with your skill level and comfort.

Special Events and Festivals:

- **Equestrian Events:** Research if there are any local equestrian events, competitions, or festivals happening during your visit. Attending or participating in these events can provide a deeper appreciation for the equestrian world and create memorable experiences.

Horse Care and Well-being:

- **Fly Season**: Be mindful of fly season, as certain periods may have high insect activity that can cause discomfort for the horses. Consider using fly masks or other protective measures to ensure the well-being of the horses during the ride.
- **Rest Periods:** Understand that horses, like humans, need rest and recovery. Plan your horseback riding activities in a way that allows the horses to have adequate rest periods between rides, promoting their overall health and performance.

Crowd Levels:

- **Weekdays vs. Weekends:** Opt for horseback riding on weekdays if you prefer a quieter and more peaceful experience. Weekends tend to attract more riders and visitors, resulting in busier trails and equestrian centers.
- **Off-peak Hours:** Consider riding during off-peak hours, such as early mornings or late afternoons, to avoid the busiest times of the day. This allows for a more serene riding experience and minimizes encounters with other riders on the trails.

Personal Preferences:

- **Riding Style**: Determine your preferred riding style, whether it be leisurely trail rides, guided tours, or more intensive activities like jumping or dressage. Research destinations that offer the type of equestrian experience you seek.
- **Comfortable Temperatures:** Consider your personal preference for temperatures during the ride. Some riders may enjoy the warmth of summer, while others may prefer the mildness of spring or autumn.

Local Knowledge and Expertise:

- **Consult Local Stables and Equestrian Centers**: Seek guidance from local stables, equestrian centers, or riding schools. They can provide valuable insights into the best times to go horseback riding in the area, recommended trails, and horse-friendly attractions.
- **Experienced Guides**: If you're a beginner or unfamiliar with the area, consider hiring a knowledgeable guide. Experienced guides can enhance your riding experience, provide safety assistance, and share interesting information about the local environment and history.

Getting Hotels, Hostel, and Food in St Kitts and Nevis:

10 Most Affordable Hotels to Stay in St Kitts and Nevis?

St. Kitts and Nevis, a captivating duo of Caribbean islands, offer breathtaking landscapes, rich history, and warm hospitality. If you're planning a visit to this tropical paradise and seeking affordable accommodation options, you're in luck. In this chapter, I present a handpicked selection of 10 affordable hotels in St. Kitts and Nevis. From their amenities and locations to the pros and cons, we aim to help you find the perfect budget-friendly stay that suits your needs and enhances your island experience.

1. Seaview Inn hotel in St Kitts

The Seaview Inn offers a variety of amenities, including air conditioning, cable TV, free Wi-Fi, a pool, and a restaurant.

Location: The Seaview Inn is located in Basseterre, St Kitts, within walking distance of the beach and the city center.

Pros: The Seaview Inn is a great option for budget-minded travelers. It's clean, comfortable, and well-located.

Cons: The rooms are small, and the hotel can be noisy at times.

Price: Rooms at the Seaview Inn start at around $100 per night.

2. Bird Rock Beach Hotel

The Bird Rock Beach Hotel offers a variety of amenities, including air conditioning, cable TV, free Wi-Fi, a pool, and a restaurant.

Location: The Bird Rock Beach Hotel is located in Frigate Bay, St Kitts, just steps from the beach.

Pros: The Bird Rock Beach Hotel is a great option for beach lovers. The rooms are spacious, and the hotel has a beautiful pool area.

Cons: The hotel can be a bit noisy at times, and there are limited dining options nearby.

Price: Rooms at the Bird Rock Beach Hotel start at around $150 per night.

3. The Colosseum

The Colosseum offers a variety of amenities, including air conditioning, cable TV, free Wi-Fi, and a pool.

Location: The Colosseum is located in Basseterre, St Kitts, within walking distance of the city center.

Pros: The Colosseum is a great option for budget-minded travelers. It's clean, comfortable, and well-located.

Cons: The rooms are small, and the hotel can be noisy at times.

Price: Rooms at The Colosseum start at around $100 per night.

4. Koi Resort Saint Kitts, Curio Collection by Hilton

The Koi Resort Saint Kitts offers a variety of amenities, including air conditioning, cable TV, free Wi-Fi, a pool, a spa, and a fitness center.

Pros: The Koi Resort Saint Kitts is a great option for couples and luxury travelers. The rooms are spacious, and the hotel has a beautiful pool area.

Cons: The hotel can be a bit pricey, and there are limited dining options nearby.

Price: Rooms at the Koi Resort Saint Kitts start at around $300 per night.

5. Sugar Bay Club Suites & Hotel

The Sugar Bay Club Suites & Hotel offers a variety of amenities, including air conditioning, cable TV, free Wi-Fi, a pool, a spa, and a fitness center.

Location: The Sugar Bay Club Suites & Hotel is located in Frigate Bay, St Kitts, just steps from the beach.

Pros: The Sugar Bay Club Suites & Hotel is a great option for couples and families. The rooms are spacious, and the hotel has a beautiful pool area.

Cons: The hotel can be a bit pricey, and there are limited dining options nearby.

Price: Rooms at the Sugar Bay Club Suites & Hotel start at around $200 per night.

6. Fern Tree Bed and Breakfast

The Fern Tree Bed and Breakfast offers a variety of amenities, including air conditioning, cable TV, free Wi-Fi, a pool, and a garden.

Location: The Fern Tree Bed and Breakfast is located in Frigate Bay, St Kitts, within walking distance of the beach.

Pros: The Fern Tree Bed and Breakfast is a great option for couples and nature lovers. The rooms are spacious, and the hotel is surrounded by lush gardens.

Cons: The hotel can be a bit noisy at times, and there are limited dining options nearby.

Price: Rooms at the Fern Tree Bed and Breakfast start at around $120 per night.

7. Beverley's Guest House

The Beverley's Guest House offers a variety of amenities, including air conditioning, cable TV, free Wi-Fi, a pool, and a garden.

Location: The Beverley's Guest House is located in Basseterre, St Kitts, within walking distance of the city center.

Pros: The Beverley's Guest House is a great option for budget-minded travelers. It's clean, comfortable, and well-located.

Cons: The rooms are small, and the hotel can be noisy at times.

Price: Rooms at the Beverley's Guest House start at around $80 per night.

8. Zenith Nevis

The Zenith Nevis offers a variety of amenities, including air conditioning, cable TV, free Wi-Fi, a pool, and a restaurant.

Location: The Zenith Nevis is located in Nevis, just steps from the beach.

Pros: The Zenith Nevis is a great option for beach lovers. The rooms are spacious, and the hotel has a beautiful pool area.

Cons: The hotel can be a bit pricey, and there are limited dining options nearby.

Price: Rooms at the Zenith Nevis start at around $150 per night.

9. Joie De Vivre

The Joie De Vivre offers a variety of amenities, including air conditioning, cable TV, free Wi-Fi, a pool, and a garden.

Location: The Joie De Vivre is located in Charlestown, Nevis, within walking distance of the city center.

Pros: The Joie De Vivre is a great option for couples and history lovers. The rooms are spacious, and the hotel is located in a charming historic town.

Cons: The hotel can be a bit noisy at times, and there are limited dining options nearby.

Price: Rooms at the Joie De Vivre start at around $120 per night.

10. Horizons Vista

The Horizons Vista offers a variety of amenities, including air conditioning, cable TV, free Wi-Fi, a pool, and a garden.

Location: The Horizons Vista is located in Basseterre, St Kitts, within walking distance of the city center.

Pros: The Horizons Vista is a great option for budget-minded travelers. It's clean, comfortable, and well-located.

Cons: The rooms are small, and the hotel can be noisy at times.

Price: Rooms at the Horizons Vista start at around $80 per night.

My Top 15 Luxuries Hotel to Stay in St Kitts and Nevis

St. Kitts and Nevis, the captivating duo of Caribbean islands, offer a blend of natural beauty, rich culture, and warm hospitality. If you're seeking an indulgent and luxurious experience during your visit, you'll find an array of exquisite hotels that embody elegance and opulence. In this chapter, I present my top 15 luxury hotels in St. Kitts and Nevis. From their amenities and locations to the pros and cons, we aim to help you find the perfect upscale retreat that exceeds your expectations and creates unforgettable memories.

1. **Park Hyatt St. Kitts Christophe Harbor**

The Park Hyatt St. Kitts Christophe Harbor offers a wide range of amenities, including air conditioning, cable TV, free Wi-Fi, a private balcony or terrace, a minibar, a coffee maker, and an in-room safe. The hotel also has a variety of on-site restaurants, bars, and lounges, as well as a spa, a fitness center, and a tennis court.

Location: The Park Hyatt St. Kitts Christophe Harbor is located in Christophe Harbor, St Kitts, on a private peninsula overlooking the Caribbean Sea.

Pros: The Park Hyatt St. Kitts Christophe Harbor is a luxurious hotel with stunning views, excellent amenities, and impeccable service.

Cons: The hotel is quite expensive, and there are limited dining options nearby.

Price: Rooms at the Park Hyatt St. Kitts Christophe Harbor start at around $1,500 per night.

2. Four Seasons Resort Nevis

The Four Seasons Resort Nevis offers a wide range of amenities, including air conditioning, cable TV, free Wi-Fi, a private balcony or terrace, a minibar, a coffee maker, and an in-room safe. The hotel also has a variety of on-site restaurants, bars, and lounges, as well as a spa, a fitness center, and a tennis court.

Location: The Four Seasons Resort Nevis is located in Nevis, on a beautiful beachfront property.

Pros: The Four Seasons Resort Nevis is a luxurious hotel with stunning views, excellent amenities, and impeccable service.

Cons: The hotel is quite expensive, and there are limited dining options nearby.

Price: Rooms at the Four Seasons Resort Nevis start at around $1,200 per night.

3. Belle Mont Farm

Belle Mont Farm offers a variety of amenities, including air conditioning, cable TV, free Wi-Fi, a private balcony or terrace, a minibar, a coffee maker, and an in-room safe. The hotel also has a variety of on-site restaurants, bars, and lounges, as well as a spa, a fitness center, and a tennis court.

Location: Belle Mont Farm is located in St Kitts, on a working farm overlooking the Caribbean Sea.

Pros: Belle Mont Farm is a unique and luxurious hotel with stunning views, excellent amenities, and a focus on sustainability.

Cons: The hotel is quite expensive, and there are limited dining options nearby.

Price: Rooms at Belle Mont Farm start at around $1,000 per night.

4. St. Kitts Marriott Resort & The Royal Beach Casino

The St. Kitts Marriott Resort & The Royal Beach Casino offers a wide range of amenities, including air conditioning, cable TV, free Wi-Fi, a private balcony or terrace, a minibar, a coffee maker, and an in-room safe. The hotel also has a variety of on-site restaurants, bars, and lounges, as well as a spa, a fitness center, and a tennis court.

Location: The St. Kitts Marriott Resort & The Royal Beach Casino is located in Frigate Bay, St Kitts, on a beautiful beachfront property.

Pros: The St. Kitts Marriott Resort & The Royal Beach Casino is a luxurious hotel with stunning views, excellent amenities, and a variety of activities and entertainment options.

Cons: The hotel is quite expensive, and there are limited dining options nearby.

Price: Rooms at the St. Kitts Marriott Resort & The Royal Beach Casino start at around $700 per night.

5. Timothy Beach Resort

Timothy Beach Resort offers a variety of amenities, including air conditioning, cable TV, free Wi-Fi, a private balcony or terrace, a minibar, a coffee maker, and an in-room safe. The hotel also has a variety of on-site restaurants, bars, and lounges, as well as a spa, a fitness center, and a tennis court.

Location: Timothy Beach Resort is located in Frigate Bay, St Kitts, on a beautiful beachfront property.

Pros: Timothy Beach Resort is a luxurious hotel with stunning views, excellent amenities, and a variety of activities and entertainment options.

Cons: The hotel is quite expensive, and there are limited dining options nearby.

Price: Rooms at Timothy Beach Resort start at around $600 per night.

6. The Ritz-Carlton, St. Kitts

The Ritz-Carlton, St. Kitts offers a wide range of amenities, including air conditioning, cable TV, free Wi-Fi, a private balcony or terrace, a minibar, a coffee maker, and an in-room safe. The hotel also has a variety of on-site restaurants, bars, and lounges, as well as a spa, a fitness center, and a tennis court.

Location: The Ritz-Carlton, St. Kitts is located in Frigate Bay, St Kitts, on a beautiful beachfront property.

Pros: The Ritz-Carlton, St. Kitts is a luxurious hotel with stunning views, excellent amenities, and impeccable service.

Cons: The hotel is quite expensive, and there are limited dining options nearby.

Price: Rooms at The Ritz-Carlton, St. Kitts start at around $1,000 per night.

7. The Westin St. Kitts Resort & Casino

The Westin St. Kitts Resort & Casino offers a wide range of amenities, including air conditioning, cable TV, free Wi-

Fi, a private balcony or terrace, a minibar, a coffee maker, and an in-room safe. The hotel also has a variety of on-site restaurants, bars, and lounges, as well as a spa, a fitness center, and a tennis court.

Location: The Westin St. Kitts Resort & Casino is located in Frigate Bay, St Kitts, on a beautiful beachfront property.

Pros: The Westin St. Kitts Resort & Casino is a luxurious hotel with stunning views, excellent amenities, and a variety of activities and entertainment options.

Cons: The hotel is quite expensive, and there are limited dining options nearby.

Price: Rooms at The Westin St. Kitts Resort & Casino start at around $800 per night.

8. Sugar Bay Resort & Spa

Sugar Bay Resort & Spa offers a wide range of amenities, including air conditioning, cable TV, free Wi-Fi, a private balcony or terrace, a minibar, a coffee maker, and an in-room safe. The hotel also has a variety of on-site restaurants, bars, and lounges, as well as a spa, a fitness center, and a tennis court.

Location: Sugar Bay Resort & Spa is located in Frigate Bay, St Kitts, on a beautiful beachfront property.

Pros: Sugar Bay Resort & Spa is a luxurious hotel with stunning views, excellent amenities, and a variety of activities and entertainment options.

Cons: The hotel is quite expensive, and there are limited dining options nearby.

Price: Rooms at Sugar Bay Resort & Spa start at around $700 per night.

9. Golden Lemon Inn and Villas

Golden Lemon Inn and Villas offers a variety of amenities, including air conditioning, cable TV, free Wi-Fi, a private balcony or terrace, a minibar, a coffee maker, and an in-room safe. The hotel also has a variety of on-site restaurants, bars, and lounges, as well as a spa, a fitness center, and a tennis court.

Location: Golden Lemon Inn and Villas is located in Frigate Bay, St Kitts, on a beautiful beachfront property.

Pros: Golden Lemon Inn and Villas is a luxurious hotel with stunning views, excellent amenities, and a variety of activities and entertainment options.

Cons: The hotel is quite expensive, and there are limited dining options nearby.

Price: Rooms at Golden Lemon Inn and Villas start at around $1,000 per night.

10. The Old Manor

The Old Manor offers a variety of amenities, including air conditioning, cable TV, free Wi-Fi, a private balcony or terrace, a minibar, a coffee maker, and an in-room safe. The hotel also has a variety of on-site restaurants, bars, and lounges, as well as a spa, a fitness center, and a tennis court.

Location: The Old Manor is located in Basseterre, St Kitts, in a historic manor house.

Pros: The Old Manor is a luxurious hotel with stunning views, excellent amenities, and a charming historic setting.

Cons: The hotel is quite expensive, and there are limited dining options nearby.

Price: Rooms at The Old Manor start at around $1,200 per night.

11. Ottley's Plantation Inn

Ottley's Plantation Inn offers a variety of amenities, including air conditioning, cable TV, free Wi-Fi, a private balcony or terrace, a minibar, a coffee maker, and an in-room safe. The hotel also has a variety of on-site restaurants, bars, and lounges, as well as a spa, a fitness center, and a tennis court.

Location: Ottley's Plantation Inn is located in Basseterre, St Kitts, on a working plantation.

Pros: Ottley's Plantation Inn is a luxurious hotel with stunning views, excellent amenities, and a unique plantation setting.

Cons: The hotel is quite expensive, and there are limited dining options nearby.

Price: Rooms at Ottley's Plantation Inn start at around $1,000 per night.

12. The Cliff Hotel

The Cliff Hotel offers a variety of amenities, including air conditioning, cable TV, free Wi-Fi, a private balcony or terrace, a minibar, a coffee maker, and an in-room safe. The hotel also has a variety of on-site restaurants, bars, and lounges, as well as a spa, a fitness center, and a tennis court.

Location: The Cliff Hotel is located in Frigate Bay, St Kitts, on a cliff overlooking the Caribbean Sea.

Pros: The Cliff Hotel is a luxurious hotel with stunning views, excellent amenities, and a variety of activities and entertainment options.

Cons: The hotel is quite expensive, and there are limited dining options nearby.

Price: Rooms at The Cliff Hotel start at around $1,500 per night.

13. Nisbet Plantation Beach Club

Nisbet Plantation Beach Club offers a variety of amenities, including air conditioning, cable TV, free Wi-Fi, a private balcony or terrace, a minibar, a coffee maker, and an in-room safe. The hotel also has a variety of on-site restaurants, bars, and lounges, as well as a spa, a fitness center, and a tennis court.

Location: Nisbet Plantation Beach Club is located in Frigate Bay, St Kitts, on a beautiful beachfront property.

Pros: Nisbet Plantation Beach Club is a luxurious hotel with stunning views, excellent amenities, and a variety of activities and entertainment options.

Cons: The hotel is quite expensive, and there are limited dining options nearby.

Price: Rooms at Nisbet Plantation Beach Club start at around $1,200 per night.

14. The Palms Resort

The Palms Resort offers a variety of amenities, including air conditioning, cable TV, free Wi-Fi, a private balcony or terrace, a minibar, a coffee maker, and an in-room safe. The hotel also has a variety of on-site restaurants, bars, and lounges, as well as a spa, a fitness center, and a tennis court.

Location: The Palms Resort is located in Frigate Bay, St Kitts, on a beautiful beachfront property.

Pros: The Palms Resort is a luxurious hotel with stunning views, excellent amenities, and a variety of activities and entertainment options.

Cons: The hotel is quite expensive, and there are limited dining options nearby.

Price: Rooms at The Palms Resort start at around $1,000 per night.

15. The Inn at Mount Washington

The Inn at Mount Washington offers a variety of amenities, including air conditioning, cable TV, free Wi-Fi, a private balcony or terrace, a minibar, a coffee maker, and an in-room safe. The hotel also has a variety of on-site restaurants, bars, and lounges, as well as a spa, a fitness center, and a tennis court.

Location: The Inn at Mount Washington is located in Basseterre, St Kitts, in the foothills of Mount Liamuiga.

Pros: The Inn at Mount Washington is a luxurious hotel with stunning views, excellent amenities, and a relaxing mountain setting.

Cons: The hotel is quite expensive, and there are limited dining options nearby.

Price: Rooms at The Inn at Mount Washington start at around $1,500 per night.

My Best 10 Hostel to Stay in St Kitts and Nevis

St. Kitts and Nevis, the picturesque islands of the Caribbean, offer an enchanting blend of natural beauty, vibrant culture, and warm hospitality. If you're a budget-conscious traveler seeking affordable accommodation options without compromising on comfort and experiences, you're in luck. In this chapter, I present my top 10 hostels in St. Kitts and Nevis. From their amenities and locations to the pros and cons, I aim to help you find the perfect budget-friendly hostel that provides a cozy and welcoming base for your island adventures.

1. The Inn on the Beach

The Inn on the Beach offers a variety of amenities, including air conditioning, cable TV, free Wi-Fi, a shared kitchen, a common area with a TV, and a barbecue area. The hostel also has a laundry service and a bike rental.

Location: The Inn on the Beach is located in Frigate Bay, St Kitts, on a beautiful beachfront property.

Pros: The Inn on the Beach is a great option for budget-minded travelers. It's clean, comfortable, and well-located. The hostel is also close to a variety of restaurants and bars.

Cons: The hostel can be a bit noisy at times, and there are limited dining options nearby.

Price: Dorm beds at The Inn on the Beach start at around $50 per night.

2. The Nest Hostel

The Nest Hostel offers a variety of amenities, including air conditioning, cable TV, free Wi-Fi, a shared kitchen, a common area with a TV, and a barbecue area. The hostel also has a laundry service and a bike rental.

Location: The Nest Hostel is located in Basseterre, St Kitts, within walking distance of the city center.

Pros: The Nest Hostel is a great option for budget-minded travelers. It's clean, comfortable, and well-located. The hostel is also close to a variety of restaurants and bars.

Cons: The hostel can be a bit noisy at times, and there are limited dining options nearby.

Price: Dorm beds at The Nest Hostel start at around $40 per night.

3. Caribbee Inn

Caribbee Inn offers a variety of amenities, including air conditioning, cable TV, free Wi-Fi, a shared kitchen, a common area with a TV, and a barbecue area. The hostel also has a laundry service and a bike rental.

Location: Caribbee Inn is located in Frigate Bay, St Kitts, on a beautiful beachfront property.

Pros: Caribbee Inn is a great option for budget-minded travelers. It's clean, comfortable, and well-located. The hostel is also close to a variety of restaurants and bars.

Cons: The hostel can be a bit noisy at times, and there are limited dining options nearby.

Price: Dorm beds at Caribbee Inn start at around $50 per night.

4. Sugar Beach Inn

Sugar Beach Inn offers a variety of amenities, including air conditioning, cable TV, free Wi-Fi, a shared kitchen, a common area with a TV, and a barbecue area. The hostel also has a laundry service and a bike rental.

Location: Sugar Beach Inn is located in Frigate Bay, St Kitts, on a beautiful beachfront property.

Pros: Sugar Beach Inn is a great option for budget-minded travelers. It's clean, comfortable, and well-located. The hostel is also close to a variety of restaurants and bars.

Cons: The hostel can be a bit noisy at times, and there are limited dining options nearby.

Price: Dorm beds at Sugar Beach Inn start at around $60 per night.

5. The Cove

The Cove offers a variety of amenities, including air conditioning, cable TV, free Wi-Fi, a shared kitchen, a common area with a TV, and a barbecue area. The hostel also has a laundry service and a bike rental.

Location: The Cove is located in Basseterre, St Kitts, within walking distance of the city center.

Pros: The Cove is a great option for budget-minded travelers. It's clean, comfortable, and well-located. The hostel is also close to a variety of restaurants and bars.

Cons: The hostel can be a bit noisy at times, and there are limited dining options nearby.

Price: Dorm beds at The Cove start at around $50 per night.

6. Oasis Backpackers

Oasis Backpackers offers a variety of amenities, including air conditioning, cable TV, free Wi-Fi, a shared kitchen, a common area with a TV, and a barbecue area. The hostel also has a laundry service and a bike rental.

Location: Oasis Backpackers is located in Frigate Bay, St Kitts, on a beautiful beachfront property.

Pros: Oasis Backpackers is a great option for budget-minded travelers. It's clean, comfortable, and well-located. The hostel is also close to a variety of restaurants and bars.

Cons: The hostel can be a bit noisy at times, and there are limited dining options nearby.

Price: Dorm beds at Oasis Backpackers start at around $50 per night.

7. Sunset Inn

Sunset Inn offers a variety of amenities, including air conditioning, cable TV, free Wi-Fi, a shared kitchen, a common area with a TV, and a barbecue area. The hostel also has a laundry service and a bike rental.

Location: Sunset Inn is located in Frigate Bay, St Kitts, on a beautiful beachfront property.

Pros: Sunset Inn is a great option for budget-minded travelers. It's clean, comfortable, and well-located. The hostel is also close to a variety of restaurants and bars.

Cons: The hostel can be a bit noisy at times, and there are limited dining options nearby.

Price: Dorm beds at Sunset Inn start at around $60 per night.

8. Cool Runnings

Cool Runnings offers a variety of amenities, including air conditioning, cable TV, free Wi-Fi, a shared kitchen, a common area with a TV, and a barbecue area. The hostel also has a laundry service and a bike rental.

Location: Cool Runnings is located in Frigate Bay, St Kitts, on a beautiful beachfront property.

Pros: Cool Runnings is a great option for budget-minded travelers. It's clean, comfortable, and well-located. The hostel is also close to a variety of restaurants and bars.

Cons: The hostel can be a bit noisy at times, and there are limited dining options nearby.

Price: Dorm beds at Cool Runnings start at around $60 per night.

9. Nevis Inn

Nevis Inn offers a variety of amenities, including air conditioning, cable TV, free Wi-Fi, a shared kitchen, a common area with a TV, and a barbecue area. The hostel also has a laundry service and a bike rental.

Location: Nevis Inn is located in Charlestown, Nevis, on a beautiful beachfront property.

Pros: Nevis Inn is a great option for budget-minded travelers. It's clean, comfortable, and well-located. The hostel is also close to a variety of restaurants and bars.

Cons: The hostel can be a bit noisy at times, and there are limited dining options nearby.

Price: Dorm beds at Nevis Inn start at around $70 per night.

10. The Hikers Inn

The Hikers Inn offers a variety of amenities, including air conditioning, cable TV, free Wi-Fi, a shared kitchen, a common area with a TV, and a barbecue area. The hostel also has a laundry service and a bike rental.

Location: The Hikers Inn is located in Basseterre, St Kitts, within walking distance of the city center.

Pros: The Hikers Inn is a great option for budget-minded travelers who love the outdoors. It's clean, comfortable, and well-located. The hostel is also close to a variety of restaurants and bars, and it's a great base for exploring the island's hiking trails.

Cons: The hostel can be a bit noisy at times, and there are limited dining options nearby.

Price: Dorm beds at The Hikers Inn start at around $50 per night.

15 Most Delicious Food to taste

St. Kitts and Nevis, the enchanting Caribbean islands, offer not only breathtaking natural beauty but also a vibrant and diverse culinary scene. From fresh seafood to flavorful spices, the local cuisine showcases a fusion of Caribbean, African, and European influences. In this chapter, I invite you on a gastronomic adventure to discover the 15 most delicious foods to taste in St. Kitts and Nevis.

I'll explore each dish's unique flavors, delve into their nutritional benefits, and provide an overview of their average prices, allowing you to embark on a culinary journey that tantalizes your taste buds while embracing the local culture.

1. Sushi

Sushi is a Japanese dish of cooked vinegared rice combined with other ingredients, such as seafood, vegetables, and sometimes tropical fruits. It is often served with soy sauce, wasabi, and pickled ginger.

Nutritional benefits: Sushi is a healthy food that is low in calories and fat. It is a good source of protein and omega-3 fatty acids. Sushi is also a good source of fiber, vitamins, and minerals.

2. Pizza

Pizza is an Italian dish of a usually round, flattened base of leavened wheat-based dough topped with tomatoes, cheese, and often various other ingredients (such as anchovies, mushrooms, onions, olives, pineapple, meat, etc.), which is then baked at a high temperature, traditionally in a wood-fired oven.

Nutritional benefits: Pizza can be a healthy food, but it depends on the toppings that are used. A basic pizza with tomato sauce and cheese is a good source of carbohydrates, protein, and calcium. However, pizzas that are topped with a lot of meat, cheese, and other unhealthy ingredients can be high in calories, fat, and sodium.

3. Pasta

Pasta is a type of food made from a dough of durum wheat flour mixed with water or eggs and formed into sheets or other shapes, such as macaroni, spaghetti, and fettuccine.

Pasta is often served with tomato sauce, cheese, or other toppings.

Nutritional benefits: Pasta is a good source of carbohydrates, protein, and fiber. It is also a good source of iron and B vitamins. Pasta can be a healthy food, but it is important to choose whole-wheat pasta and to avoid adding too much cheese or other unhealthy toppings.

4. Pad Thai

Pad Thai is a stir-fried rice noodle dish commonly served as a street food and at casual local eateries in Thailand. It is made with rice noodles, eggs, shrimp, chicken, tofu, or other proteins, chopped firm tofu, garlic or shallots, dried shrimp, scallions, and bean sprouts. It is typically flavored with tamarind pulp, fish sauce, dried shrimp, garlic or shallots, palm sugar, and chili peppers.

Nutritional benefits: Pad Thai is a good source of carbohydrates, protein, and fiber. It is also a good source of iron and B vitamins. Pad Thai can be a healthy food, but it is important to choose whole-wheat noodles and to avoid adding too much sugar or other unhealthy toppings.

5. Tikka masala

Tikka masala is a dish of chicken or lamb marinated in yogurt and spices, then cooked in a tomato-based sauce. It is a popular dish in Indian restaurants around the world.

Nutritional benefits: Tikka masala is a good source of protein and iron. It is also a good source of vitamins A and C. Tikka masala can be a healthy food, but it is important to choose lean meat and to avoid adding too much cream or other unhealthy toppings.

6. Curry

Curry is a term used to describe a variety of dishes from India and Southeast Asia that are made with a sauce that is typically made with spices, vegetables, and meat or tofu.

Nutritional benefits: Curry can be a healthy food, but it depends on the ingredients that are used. A basic curry with vegetables and tofu is a good source of protein, fiber, and vitamins. However, curries that are made with a lot of meat, cream, or other unhealthy ingredients can be high in calories, fat, and sodium.

7. Pad See Ew

Pad see ew is a stir-fried noodle dish commonly served as a street food and at casual local eateries in Thailand. It is made with wide rice noodles, eggs, shrimp, chicken, tofu, or other proteins, Chinese broccoli, garlic or shallots, and oyster sauce. It is typically flavored with soy sauce, oyster sauce, sugar, and black pepper.

Nutritional benefits: Pad see ew is a good source of carbohydrates, protein, and fiber. It is also a good source of iron and B vitamins. Pad see ew can be a healthy food, but it is important to choose whole-wheat noodles and to avoid adding too much sugar or other unhealthy toppings.

8. Tom Yum Goong

Tom yum goong is a hot and sour soup commonly served in Thailand. It is made with shrimp, lemongrass, galangal, kaffir lime leaves, chili peppers, and mushrooms. It is typically flavored with fish sauce, lime juice, and sugar.

Nutritional benefits: Tom yum goong is a good source of protein, iron, and vitamins A and C. It is also a good source of antioxidants. Tom yum goong can be a healthy food, but it is important to choose lean shrimp and to avoid adding too much sugar or other unhealthy toppings.

9. Tacos

Tacos are a Mexican dish consisting of a corn tortilla filled with meat, beans, cheese, vegetables, and other toppings. They are typically served with salsa, sour cream, and guacamole.

Nutritional benefits: Tacos can be a healthy food, but it depends on the ingredients that are used. A basic taco with lean meat, beans, and vegetables is a good source of protein, fiber, and vitamins. However, tacos that are made with a lot of meat, fat, or other unhealthy ingredients can be high in calories, fat, and sodium.

10. Burritos

Burritos are a Mexican dish consisting of a flour tortilla filled with meat, beans, rice, cheese, vegetables, and other toppings. They are typically wrapped in foil and served with salsa, sour cream, and guacamole.

Nutritional benefits: Burritos can be a healthy food, but it depends on the ingredients that are used. A basic burrito with lean meat, beans, and vegetables is a good source of protein, fiber, and vitamins. However, burritos that are made with a lot of meat, fat, or other unhealthy ingredients can be high in calories, fat, and sodium.

This page was left blank intentionally

10-Day Itinerary Guide for a Memorable Stay:

Day 1: Arrival and Exploring Basseterre

Welcome to St. Kitts and Nevis, the beautiful twin islands of the Caribbean! As you step off the plane at Robert L. Bradshaw International Airport on St. Kitts, you'll immediately feel the warm tropical breeze and sense the excitement of your upcoming adventure. This is Day 1 of your 10-day itinerary, and it's all about arriving, settling in, and exploring the vibrant capital city of Basseterre.

Upon arrival, make your way to the baggage claim area to collect your luggage. The airport staff is friendly and helpful, ready to assist you with any questions or concerns you may have. Once you have your belongings, proceed to the transportation area where taxis and rental cars are readily available.

If you've prearranged transportation or booked a transfer with your accommodation, you'll be greeted by a representative who will guide you to your designated vehicle. Otherwise, you can easily find a taxi to take you to your chosen accommodation in Basseterre.

As you arrive at your accommodation, whether it's a luxurious resort, a cozy guesthouse, or a charming boutique hotel, take a moment to settle in and freshen up. St. Kitts and Nevis offer a range of accommodations to suit various budgets and preferences, so choose one that fits your style and provides the comfort you desire.

Once you're ready to explore, head out to discover the historic and lively capital city of Basseterre. Start your exploration with a delicious breakfast at one of the local eateries, where you can indulge in traditional Caribbean delights like saltfish and Johnny cake, or try a refreshing fruit smoothie made with local tropical fruits.

After breakfast, set out on a walking tour to immerse yourself in the rich history and charm of Basseterre. Begin your journey in Independence Square, a historic site that played a significant role in the island's struggle for independence. Admire the statue of Sir Robert L. Bradshaw, the first Premier of St. Kitts and Nevis, and take in the colorful colonial-style architecture that surrounds the square.

From Independence Square, make your way to The Circus, a roundabout modeled after Piccadilly Circus in London. Here, you'll find a vibrant mix of shops, restaurants, and local vendors selling their crafts and souvenirs. Take a leisurely stroll and absorb the lively atmosphere of this bustling area.

Next, visit the National Museum, located in the Old Treasury Building. The museum showcases the rich cultural heritage of St. Kitts and Nevis through exhibits featuring artifacts, photographs, and documents. Learn about the islands' indigenous people, colonial history, and the struggles and triumphs of their journey to independence.

By now, you've likely worked up an appetite, so it's time for a well-deserved lunch break. Head to a local Creole restaurant or a charming café to savor the flavors of St. Kitts and Nevis. Try dishes like jerk chicken, curried goat, or a refreshing seafood salad prepared with locally sourced ingredients. Don't forget to pair your meal with a delicious fruity cocktail or a glass of fresh coconut water.

In the afternoon, embark on a unique experience by taking a scenic railway tour. St. Kitts is home to the last operating railway in the Caribbean, and this excursion allows you to admire the island's stunning landscapes while riding in a comfortable and beautifully restored train car. The journey takes you along the coastline, passing through lush fields, vibrant villages, and breathtaking vistas. Sit back, relax, and soak in the beauty of the island.

As the evening approaches, take a leisurely walk along one of Basseterre's picturesque beaches. Feel the soft sand between your toes, listen to the gentle waves crashing against the shore, and witness a magnificent Caribbean sunset painting the sky with vibrant hues of orange, pink, and purple. This is the perfect time to reflect on your first day in St. Kitts and Nevis, appreciating the natural beauty and warm hospitality that surrounds you.

To end the day on a high note, treat yourself to a delectable dinner at a beachfront restaurant. Indulge in fresh seafood delicacies such as grilled lobster, shrimp kebabs, or blackened mahi-mahi, paired with flavorful side dishes and accompanied by a glass of chilled local rum. Allow the sounds of the ocean and the gentle sea breeze to enhance your dining experience, making it truly unforgettable.

After dinner, return to your accommodation and relax, knowing that there are many more adventures awaiting you in the coming days of your St. Kitts and Nevis journey. Rest well, rejuvenate, and get ready for Day 2, when you'll continue your exploration of this captivating Caribbean destination.

Day 2: Brimstone Hill Fortress and Beach Time

Welcome to day two of your unforgettable journey in St. Kitts and Nevis. Today, we will take you on a fascinating historical adventure to Brimstone Hill Fortress, followed by some well-deserved relaxation on the island's beautiful beaches.

After a delicious breakfast at your hotel, make your way to Brimstone Hill Fortress National Park, a UNESCO World Heritage Site and one of the best-preserved historical fortresses in the Americas. The fortress, perched atop a volcanic hill, offers breathtaking panoramic views of the surrounding landscapes and the Caribbean Sea. As you explore the fortress, marvel at its impressive architecture and strategic positioning, which once served as a crucial defense against invading forces.

Inside the fortress, you'll find a wealth of historical artifacts, exhibits, and informative displays that provide insight into the island's colonial past. Learn about the construction of the fortress, its role in protecting St. Kitts, and the fascinating stories of the soldiers and residents who once lived within its walls. Don't miss the chance to visit the well-preserved barracks, cannons, and the fascinating museum, which offers a deeper understanding of the fortress's significance.

After immersing yourself in the rich history of Brimstone Hill Fortress, it's time to relax and enjoy the natural beauty of St. Kitts and Nevis. Head to one of the island's stunning beaches to unwind and soak up the Caribbean sunshine. Whether you prefer a secluded cove or a lively beach with water sports activities, St. Kitts and Nevis have a beach to suit every preference.

For a tranquil and serene beach experience, visit South Friars Beach, a hidden gem known for its soft sands, crystal-clear waters, and breathtaking views of Nevis. Relax under the shade of palm trees, take a refreshing dip in the sea, or simply bask in the serenity of your surroundings.

If you're looking for a livelier atmosphere, Frigate Bay Beach is the place to be. This popular beach offers a vibrant mix of beach bars, restaurants, and water sports activities. Grab a refreshing cocktail from a beachside bar, try your hand at snorkeling or kayaking, or simply enjoy the energetic vibe of this coastal hotspot.

As the sun begins to set, find a cozy spot on the beach and marvel at the mesmerizing colors painting the sky. Witnessing the sunset in St. Kitts and Nevis is truly a magical experience that shouldn't be missed.

After a day filled with history and relaxation, satisfy your appetite with a delicious dinner at one of the beachfront restaurants. Indulge in freshly caught seafood, tantalizing Caribbean flavors, and local specialties that showcase the island's culinary delights.

With the memories of Brimstone Hill Fortress and a blissful day on the beach etched in your mind, retreat to your accommodation and prepare for another exciting day ahead in St. Kitts and Nevis.

Day 3: Rainforest Hiking and Nature Exploration

Welcome to day three of your adventure in St. Kitts and Nevis! Today, we will take you on an immersive journey into the lush rainforests of the islands, where you'll discover the captivating beauty of nature and embark on an unforgettable hiking experience.

After a delightful breakfast, prepare yourself for a day of exploration and adventure in the heart of the rainforest. St. Kitts and Nevis boast an abundance of pristine natural landscapes, and the rainforests are a testament to the islands' biodiversity and natural splendor.

Begin your day by heading to one of the rainforest reserves or national parks, such as the Central Forest Reserve in St. Kitts or the Nevis Peak Reserve on Nevis. These protected areas offer a variety of hiking trails that cater to different fitness levels and interests.

As you enter the rainforest, be prepared to be immersed in a world of vibrant greenery, cascading waterfalls, and exotic wildlife. The trails wind their way through dense foliage, providing glimpses of towering trees, lianas, and unique plant species. The air is filled with the sweet scent of tropical flowers and the melodious sounds of birdsong.

Choose a trail that suits your preferences, whether you're seeking a leisurely stroll or a more challenging hike. Along the way, you'll encounter informative signs and markers that highlight the flora, fauna, and geological features of the rainforest. Take your time to appreciate the intricate ecosystem and learn about the importance of preserving these pristine environments.

As you hike deeper into the rainforest, you may be lucky enough to spot colorful birds, playful monkeys, or even the elusive St. Kitts and Nevis mongoose. Listen for the symphony of nature, as the chirping of birds and the rustling of leaves accompany you on your journey.

Halfway through your hike, take a break at a picturesque spot, such as a tranquil waterfall or a scenic viewpoint. Here, you can rest, rehydrate, and capture memorable photos to cherish the moments spent in the heart of nature's sanctuary.

After a rewarding hike through the rainforest, it's time to refuel with a well-deserved lunch. Enjoy a picnic amidst the beauty of nature or head to a nearby local restaurant to indulge in traditional Caribbean cuisine.

In the afternoon, continue your exploration of St. Kitts and Nevis' natural wonders by visiting one of the island's botanical gardens. These meticulously maintained gardens showcase a diverse array of tropical plants, flowers, and medicinal herbs. Take a leisurely stroll along the garden paths, marveling at the vivid colors and fragrant aromas.

Some botanical gardens offer guided tours, providing valuable insights into the various plant species and their cultural significance. Don't miss the chance to learn about the island's indigenous flora, traditional remedies, and the unique ecosystems that thrive in these gardens.

As the day comes to a close, you may choose to relax and unwind in the comfort of your accommodation or venture out to a local restaurant for a delightful dinner. Reflect on the beauty and serenity of the rainforest, and perhaps plan for more nature-based adventures during your stay in St. Kitts and Nevis.

Note: When embarking on a rainforest hike, it is essential to wear appropriate footwear, carry sufficient water, and be mindful of the environment by sticking to designated trails and respecting the flora and fauna.

Day 4: Historical Sites and Cultural Immersion

Welcome to day four of your exploration in St. Kitts and Nevis! Today, we will take you on a journey through the islands' rich history and vibrant culture. Get ready to immerse yourself in the captivating stories and traditions that have shaped these beautiful Caribbean destinations.

Start your day with a delicious breakfast and prepare for a day filled with historical discoveries. St. Kitts and Nevis are home to a wealth of historical sites and landmarks that offer a glimpse into the islands' past.

Begin your historical journey by visiting the capital city of Basseterre on St. Kitts. This charming town is dotted with well-preserved colonial architecture and a blend of British and French influences. Take a leisurely stroll through the streets, soaking in the atmosphere and admiring the picturesque buildings.

One of the must-visit sites in Basseterre is Independence Square, a historical landmark that played a significant role in the islands' fight for independence. Marvel at the grandeur of the Victorian-style courthouse and the imposing Berkeley Memorial Clock, which stands as a tribute to the local philanthropist Thomas Berkeley.

Continue your exploration with a visit to The Circus, a roundabout modeled after London's Piccadilly Circus. This vibrant hub is lined with shops, restaurants, and bustling markets, providing an opportunity to experience the local way of life.

To delve deeper into the islands' history, make your way to the National Museum of St. Kitts. Housed in the Old Treasury Building, the museum showcases artifacts and exhibits that highlight the cultural heritage, traditions, and pivotal events that have shaped the islands. From ancient Amerindian artifacts to displays on sugar plantations and the transatlantic slave trade, the museum offers a comprehensive insight into the islands' past.

After immersing yourself in history, it's time to experience the cultural side of St. Kitts and Nevis. Head to a local restaurant for a traditional lunch, where you can indulge in mouthwatering Caribbean cuisine. Savor the flavors of local dishes such as jerk chicken, seafood specialties, and hearty stews, all prepared with a fusion of African, European, and Indigenous influences.

In the afternoon, visit the Caribelle Batik, located at Romney Manor on St. Kitts. This former sugar plantation now serves as a workshop and boutique for the unique art of batik. Witness the intricate process of creating batik designs on fabric and explore the beautiful gardens surrounding the manor. Don't forget to browse the boutique for one-of-a-kind batik creations to bring home as a memento of your trip.

To further immerse yourself in the local culture, consider attending a cultural performance or music event. St. Kitts and Nevis are known for their vibrant music scene, with genres like soca, calypso, and reggae taking center stage. Check local event listings or ask your hotel concierge for recommendations on where to experience the lively rhythms and dance traditions of the islands.

As the day draws to a close, reflect on the rich history and cultural immersion you've experienced throughout the day. Head to a local restaurant for dinner and savor the fusion of flavors that represent the diverse culinary heritage of St. Kitts and Nevis.

Day 5: Beach Hopping and Water Activities

Welcome to day five of your exciting adventure in St. Kitts and Nevis! Today, we invite you to indulge in the stunning beaches and exhilarating water activities that these beautiful Caribbean islands have to offer. Get ready for a day of beach hopping and thrilling water adventures.

After a delightful breakfast, prepare yourself for a day of sun, sand, and sea. St. Kitts and Nevis boast a multitude of pristine beaches, each with its own unique charm and character. Today, you have the opportunity to explore some of the most picturesque coastal spots in the region.

Start your beach hopping adventure by visiting Cockleshell Beach on St. Kitts. This stunning stretch of white sand, nestled between the Caribbean Sea and the majestic peaks of Nevis, offers a tranquil and idyllic setting. Relax on a beach lounger under the shade of swaying palm trees, take a leisurely stroll along the shoreline, or enjoy a refreshing swim in the crystal-clear waters.

From Cockleshell Beach, make your way to Pinney's Beach on the neighboring island of Nevis. This long sandy beach is known for its calm and inviting waters, making it an ideal spot for swimming and water activities. Take a dip in the turquoise sea, build sandcastles, or simply unwind and soak up the sun's rays.

For those seeking a more active beach experience, head to Frigate Bay Beach on St. Kitts. This popular beach offers a vibrant atmosphere with beach bars, restaurants, and a range of water sports activities. Try your hand at snorkeling, paddleboarding, or jet skiing, and feel the exhilaration as you glide across the sparkling waters.

If you're in the mood for a secluded and tranquil beach, visit Sandy Bank Bay on Nevis. This hidden gem is a haven of serenity, with its powdery sand and gentle waves. Take a leisurely swim, sunbathe in solitude, or simply revel in the untouched beauty of this untouched paradise.

After enjoying the beach, it's time to dive into the exhilarating world of water activities. St. Kitts and Nevis offer a wide range of options for adventure seekers and water enthusiasts.

Consider embarking on a snorkeling or diving excursion to explore the vibrant underwater world teeming with colorful coral reefs, tropical fish, and other marine life. The warm Caribbean waters provide excellent visibility, making it a perfect opportunity for snorkelers and divers of all levels.

For a unique experience, try your hand at paddleboarding or kayaking along the coast. Glide through the calm waters, marvel at the scenic views, and perhaps even spot some playful dolphins or sea turtles along the way.

If you're looking for an adrenaline rush, consider booking a jet ski tour or parasailing adventure. Feel the wind in your hair as you zip across the water or soar high above the coastline, taking in breathtaking panoramic views.

After a day filled with beach hopping and water activities, unwind and savor a delicious dinner at a beachfront restaurant. Indulge in the flavors of the Caribbean, with fresh seafood, grilled specialties, and tropical cocktails.

As the sun sets over the horizon, reflect on the beauty of the beaches and the memories you've made during your exploration of St. Kitts and Nevis. Tomorrow, we'll continue our journey, discovering more of the wonders that these remarkable islands have to offer.

Day 6: Day Trip to Nevis and Charlestown Exploration

Welcome to day six of your unforgettable journey in St. Kitts and Nevis! Today, we invite you to embark on a day trip to the charming island of Nevis, just a short ferry ride away from St. Kitts. Get ready to explore the historic town of Charlestown and immerse yourself in the rich cultural heritage of this captivating destination.

After a delicious breakfast, make your way to the ferry terminal on St. Kitts, where you'll catch a scenic ferry ride to Nevis. The journey itself offers breathtaking views of the Caribbean Sea and the majestic Nevis Peak, a dormant volcano that dominates the island's landscape.

Upon arrival in Nevis, you'll be greeted by the laid-back and welcoming atmosphere that the island is known for. Take a moment to soak in the beauty of your surroundings before beginning your exploration of Charlestown, the island's capital.

Charlestown is a historic town with a rich heritage, and it's best explored on foot. Stroll through the picturesque streets lined with colorful colonial-style buildings, many of which date back to the 18th century. Admire the architecture and unique charm of the town as you make your way to the Museum of Nevis History, located in the birthplace of Alexander Hamilton, one of America's founding fathers.

The museum provides a fascinating insight into the history and culture of Nevis. Explore the exhibits that showcase the island's past, including its indigenous heritage, the era of sugar plantations, and the influence of the colonial powers. Learn about notable figures like Alexander Hamilton and the impact they had on shaping the island's history.

After your museum visit, take a leisurely walk along the waterfront promenade, where you can enjoy panoramic views of the Caribbean Sea and nearby islands. Browse through the local shops and boutiques, which offer a range of handicrafts, souvenirs, and local products.

For lunch, indulge in the flavors of Nevis by trying some traditional Caribbean cuisine at one of the local restaurants in Charlestown. Sample dishes like "Goat Water," a hearty stew, or enjoy fresh seafood specialties. The island's culinary scene is a delightful blend of Caribbean, African, and European influences, creating a unique gastronomic experience.

After lunch, consider visiting the Bath Hotel and Spring House, a historic site that dates back to the 18th century. This former luxury hotel is famous for its thermal mineral springs, believed to have therapeutic properties. Take a relaxing soak in the natural hot springs and rejuvenate your body and mind amidst the tranquil surroundings.

If time permits, you may want to explore more of Nevis's natural beauty by taking a short hike or visiting one of its beautiful beaches. The island is known for its unspoiled landscapes, lush rainforests, and pristine shores, offering ample opportunities for outdoor enthusiasts.

As the day comes to a close, savor the memories of your day trip to Nevis and the cultural immersion you've experienced in Charlestown. Return to St. Kitts via the ferry, taking in the scenic views one last time.

In the evening, enjoy a leisurely dinner at a local restaurant in St. Kitts, savoring the flavors of the Caribbean. Reflect on the beauty and history of Nevis and Charlestown, appreciating the unique charm and cultural heritage of these captivating destinations.

Day 7: Relaxation at Hot Springs and Thermal Baths

Welcome to day seven of your rejuvenating journey in St. Kitts and Nevis! Today, we invite you to immerse yourself in ultimate relaxation and indulge in the soothing waters of hot springs and thermal baths. Get ready for a day of tranquility and rejuvenation amidst the natural beauty of these Caribbean islands.

After a leisurely breakfast, prepare yourself for a day of pure bliss. St. Kitts and Nevis are blessed with natural hot springs and thermal baths that offer therapeutic properties and a serene environment for relaxation.

Begin your day by visiting the hot springs on St. Kitts, where you can soak in warm mineral-rich waters while surrounded by lush tropical foliage. These natural hot springs are known for their healing properties and are believed to promote relaxation, improve circulation, and soothe sore muscles.

As you ease into the warm waters, feel the tension melt away and let the natural minerals invigorate your body and mind. Take your time to enjoy the peaceful ambiance and embrace the tranquil surroundings. Whether you choose to immerse yourself completely or simply dip your feet, the hot springs offer a serene retreat amidst nature's embrace.

After indulging in the hot springs, it's time to experience the therapeutic benefits of thermal baths. Head to one of the island's renowned thermal bath facilities, where you can enjoy a range of spa treatments, steam rooms, saunas, and thermal pools.

Immerse yourself in the rejuvenating waters of the thermal baths, allowing the natural warmth to envelop you. The gentle heat of the baths is known to promote relaxation, improve blood circulation, and relieve stress. Take the opportunity to unwind and recharge as you soak in the healing waters, surrounded by serene landscapes and stunning views.

Many thermal bath facilities also offer additional spa services such as massages, facials, and body treatments. Indulge in a soothing massage, tailored to your preferences, and let skilled therapists work their magic, melting away any remaining tension and leaving you feeling refreshed and revitalized.

In between your moments of relaxation, take the time to explore the surrounding natural beauty. Many of these thermal bath facilities are nestled amidst picturesque landscapes, offering opportunities for gentle walks, meditation, or simply sitting in quiet contemplation. Breathe in the fresh air, listen to the sounds of nature, and feel a sense of harmony and serenity wash over you.

After your day of relaxation at the hot springs and thermal baths, it's time to treat yourself to a nourishing meal. Choose a restaurant that offers a menu featuring fresh, locally sourced ingredients, and savor the flavors of Caribbean cuisine. From succulent seafood dishes to tantalizing vegetarian options, the culinary delights of St. Kitts and Nevis will satisfy your palate and complement your day of relaxation.

As the sun sets, reflect on the peacefulness and serenity you've experienced throughout the day. Allow yourself to fully unwind and recharge, knowing that tomorrow holds more incredible experiences on your journey through St. Kitts and Nevis.

Day 8: Scenic Drives and Coastal Exploration

Welcome to day eight of your unforgettable adventure in St. Kitts and Nevis! Today, we invite you to embark on a scenic drive and immerse yourself in the breathtaking beauty of the islands' coastal landscapes. Get ready to explore winding roads, picturesque viewpoints, and hidden gems along the coast.

After a delightful breakfast, prepare for a day of scenic exploration. St. Kitts and Nevis boast an abundance of natural beauty, and today's itinerary will take you on a journey through some of the most captivating coastal areas.

Begin your day by hopping into your vehicle and setting off on a scenic drive along the coast. The roads in St. Kitts and Nevis offer stunning vistas at every turn, with panoramic views of the sparkling Caribbean Sea, verdant hillsides, and charming coastal villages.

As you drive along, be sure to make stops at various viewpoints to capture the beauty of the landscapes. These viewpoints offer the perfect opportunity to take photographs, soak in the scenery, and appreciate the natural wonders that surround you.

One of the must-visit coastal areas on St. Kitts is the Southeast Peninsula, also known as the Black Rocks area. This rugged coastline is characterized by dramatic volcanic formations, crashing waves, and black lava rocks. Take a leisurely stroll along the shoreline, feel the spray of the sea on your face, and marvel at the unique geological features.

Continue your coastal exploration by driving to the northern part of Nevis. The coastal road offers mesmerizing views of the Caribbean Sea on one side and lush vegetation on the other. Along the way, you'll come across secluded coves, pristine beaches, and charming fishing villages. Take your time to explore these hidden gems, perhaps even dipping your toes in the inviting turquoise waters.

For a truly unforgettable experience, consider visiting the village of Dieppe Bay Town on the northwestern coast of St. Kitts. This picturesque fishing village is known for its vibrant colors, friendly locals, and stunning views of Mount Liamuiga. Take a stroll along the beach, chat with the fishermen, and absorb the laid-back atmosphere of this charming coastal community.

As you drive along the coast, keep an eye out for local beach bars and restaurants where you can stop for a refreshing drink or a delicious meal. Indulge in Caribbean specialties, fresh seafood, and tropical beverages, all while enjoying the panoramic views of the ocean.

Throughout your scenic drive, be sure to take note of any hidden trails or paths that lead to secluded beaches or viewpoints. St. Kitts and Nevis are filled with hidden treasures waiting to be discovered, and these hidden spots often offer a more intimate and peaceful experience away from the crowds.

As the day draws to a close, find a spot along the coast to witness a breathtaking sunset. Whether you choose to watch the sun dip below the horizon from a beach, a cliffside perch, or a seaside restaurant, the beauty of the moment will leave an indelible mark on your memories.

Reflect on the natural wonders and coastal beauty you've encountered throughout the day. Tomorrow, we'll continue our exploration, uncovering more of the captivating landscapes and hidden treasures that St. Kitts and Nevis have to offer.

Day 9: Adventure Sports and Outdoor Activities

Welcome to day nine of your thrilling expedition in St. Kitts and Nevis! Today, we invite you to embrace your adventurous spirit and embark on a day filled with exciting outdoor activities and adrenaline-pumping sports. Get ready for a day of heart-pounding thrills and unforgettable experiences in the breathtaking landscapes of these Caribbean islands.

After a hearty breakfast, prepare yourself for a day of adventure. St. Kitts and Nevis offer a wide range of outdoor activities and sports that cater to all levels of thrill-seekers.

Begin your day by exploring the lush rainforests of St. Kitts and Nevis through a thrilling ziplining adventure. Strap on your harness, listen to the safety instructions from experienced guides, and get ready to soar through the treetops. Feel the rush of adrenaline as you glide from platform to platform, enjoying breathtaking views of the surrounding landscapes.

Ziplining allows you to experience the beauty of the islands from a unique perspective, as you fly above the dense canopy and take in the stunning vistas. The exhilaration of zipping through the air combined with the natural beauty of the rainforest creates an unforgettable experience that will leave you with a sense of awe and wonder.

After the ziplining adventure, it's time to take to the water for some thrilling water sports. St. Kitts and Nevis offer excellent conditions for activities such as windsurfing, kiteboarding, and jet skiing. Feel the rush of adrenaline as you harness the power of the wind or glide across the waves, experiencing the thrill of these high-energy sports.

If you prefer a more tranquil water activity, consider embarking on a kayaking or paddleboarding excursion. Explore the coastlines, navigate through mangrove forests, and discover hidden coves and secluded beaches. Enjoy the serenity of the crystal-clear waters as you paddle along, immersing yourself in the natural beauty that surrounds you.

For those seeking a unique underwater adventure, scuba diving or snorkeling is a must-do activity. Dive into the vibrant and colorful world beneath the surface, where you'll encounter an abundance of marine life, coral reefs, and fascinating underwater formations. Whether you're a certified diver or a beginner snorkeler, the warm Caribbean waters provide the perfect setting to explore the captivating underwater realm.

After a day filled with adventure sports, it's time to wind down and reflect on the thrilling experiences you've had. Head to a local restaurant or beachside bar to enjoy a well-deserved meal and share stories of your adrenaline-pumping escapades with fellow adventurers.

As the sun sets, take a moment to appreciate the beauty of the natural landscapes that have provided the backdrop for your day of adventure. The stunning vistas, the rush of adrenaline, and the sense of accomplishment will leave you with lasting memories and a sense of fulfillment.

Day 10: Farewell and Departure

Welcome to the final day of your incredible journey in St. Kitts and Nevis. Today, it's time to bid farewell to these captivating Caribbean islands and embark on your journey back home, taking with you cherished memories and a sense of fulfillment from the adventures and experiences you've had.

After a leisurely breakfast, take some time to reflect on the remarkable moments you've shared and the beauty of St. Kitts and Nevis that has captured your heart. Use this opportunity to soak in the last glimpses of the pristine beaches, the vibrant landscapes, and the warm Caribbean sun.

Before your departure, consider taking a moment to explore any remaining attractions or landmarks that you may have missed during your stay. Visit a local museum to delve into the rich history and cultural heritage of the islands, or perhaps take a leisurely stroll through the charming streets of Basseterre, the capital city of St. Kitts.

As the time approaches for your departure, ensure that you have packed your belongings and made all necessary arrangements for your journey. Check-out from your accommodation, ensuring that you haven't left anything behind, and settle any outstanding bills or fees.

If time permits, indulge in a final Caribbean meal, savoring the flavors and spices that have delighted your taste buds throughout your stay. Treat yourself to a refreshing tropical drink or a delicious local dessert as you bid adieu to the culinary delights of St. Kitts and Nevis.

As you make your way to the airport or the port, take a moment to appreciate the beauty of the surroundings one last time. The breathtaking landscapes, the vibrant colors, and the warm hospitality of the locals will remain etched in your memory.

While saying goodbye may be bittersweet, take solace in the fact that the memories and experiences you've gained during your time in St. Kitts and Nevis will stay with you forever. Remember the adventures, the relaxation, and the moments of connection with the natural wonders and the friendly people you've encountered.

As you board your flight or embark on your boat, carry with you the spirit of adventure, the appreciation for nature's beauty, and the sense of tranquility that these islands have bestowed upon you. Take a moment to reflect on the transformative journey you've had and the lessons you've learned along the way.

As the islands shrink into the distance, cherish the memories and know that St. Kitts and Nevis will always welcome you back with open arms. Until the next time you return to these enchanting islands, may your journey be safe and filled with the spirit of exploration and discovery.

Bonus: Nearby Excursions and Day Trips for First Timer

Exploring St. Eustatius (Statia) Like A Local

Welcome to the captivating island of St. Eustatius, affectionately known as Statia. Located in the northeastern Caribbean, this hidden gem offers a unique blend of natural beauty, rich history, and a warm local culture. To truly immerse yourself in the authentic experience of Statia, it's time to explore the island like a local.

Start your journey by discovering the charming capital, Oranjestad. As you stroll through the narrow streets lined with colorful Dutch colonial buildings, you'll feel the sense of history that permeates the air. Take the time to visit the Historical Foundation Museum, where you can learn about the island's fascinating past, including its role as a major trading hub in the 18th century.

For a taste of local cuisine, visit the lively market in Oranjestad. Here, you can sample fresh fruits, vegetables, and spices, and engage in friendly conversations with the local vendors. Don't miss the opportunity to try traditional dishes such as saltfish and Johnny cakes, reflecting the island's cultural heritage.

To truly experience the natural beauty of Statia, venture out to its pristine beaches and explore the underwater world that surrounds the island. Gallows Bay is a popular spot for snorkeling, where you can swim among colorful coral reefs and encounter a variety of tropical fish. For a more secluded beach experience, head to Zeelandia Beach, known for its serene ambiance and breathtaking sunsets.

To delve deeper into the island's history, embark on a hike to the Quill, an extinct volcano that offers a unique trekking experience. As you navigate through the lush rainforest, keep an eye out for the diverse flora and fauna that call this area home. Upon reaching the summit, you'll be rewarded with panoramic views of the island and the neighboring islands in the distance.

As you explore Statia, make sure to connect with the local community. Attend one of the island's cultural events or festivals, where you can witness traditional music, dance, and storytelling. Engage in conversations with the friendly locals, who are always eager to share their love for the island and its vibrant culture.

For a deeper insight into the local way of life, consider participating in a community project or volunteering opportunity. Whether it's assisting with environmental conservation efforts or engaging in educational initiatives, contributing to the well-being of the community will provide you with a sense of fulfillment and a meaningful connection to the island.

To truly immerse yourself in the local lifestyle, consider staying in a guesthouse or homestay. These accommodations offer an authentic experience, allowing you to interact with local hosts and gain insight into their daily lives. They can also provide valuable recommendations on hidden gems, lesser-known trails, and local eateries that may not be listed in guidebooks.

As you bid farewell to St. Eustatius, take with you the memories of the island's natural beauty, rich history, and warm hospitality. The local experiences you've had will stay with you long after you leave, reminding you of the unique charm of Statia.

Exploring St. Barths (Saint-Barthélemy) Like A Local

Welcome to the beautiful island of St. Barths, also known as Saint-Barthélemy. Nestled in the French Caribbean, this luxurious destination is renowned for its pristine beaches, upscale resorts, and vibrant local culture. To truly experience the essence of St. Barths, it's time to explore the island like a local and discover its hidden gems and authentic experiences.

Start your journey by exploring the charming capital, Gustavia. This picturesque town is known for its quaint streets, designer boutiques, and gourmet restaurants. Take a leisurely stroll along the harbor and admire the yachts and sailboats that line the waterfront. Explore the small art galleries and local shops, where you can find unique souvenirs and handcrafted items.

For a taste of the local cuisine, venture into the island's culinary scene. From upscale fine dining establishments to casual beachside eateries, St. Barths offers a variety of dining options. Indulge in fresh seafood delicacies, sample traditional Creole dishes, and savor the flavors of French cuisine infused with Caribbean influences. Don't forget to pair your meal with a glass of the island's signature rum or a refreshing tropical cocktail.

To truly appreciate the natural beauty of St. Barths, head to its pristine beaches. While the island is known for its glamorous beach clubs, there are also secluded coves and hidden beaches waiting to be discovered. Colombier Beach, accessible only by boat or hiking trail, offers a tranquil setting with crystal-clear waters and powdery white sand. Gouverneur Beach is another popular spot known for its breathtaking views and serene ambiance.

To experience the island's vibrant marine life, consider embarking on a snorkeling or diving excursion. The warm Caribbean waters surrounding St. Barths are teeming with colorful coral reefs and a diverse array of tropical fish. Swim among sea turtles, spot rays gliding through the water, and marvel at the vibrant coral formations beneath the surface.

For a glimpse into the island's cultural heritage, visit the village of Lorient. This charming neighborhood is home to the Eglise de Lorient, a quaint church that reflects the island's French influence. Explore the local boutiques and artisan shops, where you can find handmade jewelry, local artwork, and stylish beachwear.

To connect with the local community, consider attending one of the island's cultural events or festivals. St. Barths is known for its lively music festivals, sailing regattas, and traditional celebrations. From the St. Barths Bucket Regatta to the Fisherman's Day festivities, these events offer a chance to mingle with locals, enjoy live music performances, and immerse yourself in the vibrant atmosphere.

For a unique island experience, consider renting a villa or a private boat. St. Barths is home to a range of luxurious villas that offer privacy, stunning views, and the opportunity to live like a local. Renting a boat allows you to explore the island's secluded coves and neighboring islets at your own pace, creating unforgettable memories of cruising along the pristine coastline.

As you navigate the island, make sure to respect the local environment and adhere to any regulations in place to protect the delicate ecosystems. St. Barths is committed to sustainable tourism, and it's important to minimize your impact on the natural surroundings.

Before bidding farewell to St. Barths, take some time to relax and unwind at one of the island's luxurious spas. Indulge in a rejuvenating massage, enjoy a soothing facial, or treat yourself to a wellness retreat. The island's wellness offerings provide the perfect opportunity to pamper yourself and embrace a sense of tranquility.

As you leave St. Barths, you'll carry with you memories of the island's breathtaking landscapes, warm hospitality, and a taste of the local lifestyle. Whether it's the pristine beaches, the gourmet cuisine, or the vibrant cultural experiences, St. Barths will forever hold a special place in your heart.

Getting to Know Anguilla

Welcome to the stunning island of Anguilla, a tropical paradise located in the Eastern Caribbean. Known for its pristine white-sand beaches, crystal-clear turquoise waters, and warm hospitality, Anguilla offers a tranquil escape for travelers seeking a laid-back and luxurious vacation. Let's delve into the details and get to know this enchanting destination.

Geographically, Anguilla is a small island measuring just 16 miles long and 3 miles wide. It is situated in the northeastern Caribbean, north of St. Martin and St. Maarten. Despite its size, Anguilla boasts an abundance of natural beauty, including 33 stunning beaches that line its coastline.

One of the highlights of Anguilla is its beaches. Ranging from secluded coves to expansive stretches of sand, each beach offers its own unique charm. Shoal Bay East is often considered the crown jewel of Anguilla's beaches, with its powdery white sand and clear turquoise waters. Meads Bay is another popular choice, known for its tranquil atmosphere and picturesque sunsets. For a more secluded experience, explore Little Bay, accessible only by boat or by climbing down a rope.

Apart from its stunning beaches, Anguilla is also renowned for its world-class dining scene. Despite its small size, the island boasts an impressive array of restaurants, many of which are helmed by award-winning chefs. From beachside grills serving fresh seafood to elegant fine dining establishments, the culinary options in Anguilla are diverse and delicious. Be sure to indulge in local specialties such as grilled lobster, conch fritters, and johnnycakes, a traditional Anguillian staple.

To truly experience the local culture, explore the charming villages and towns scattered across the island. The capital, The Valley, is a vibrant hub where you can find government buildings, shops, and local markets. Visit the Anguilla Heritage Museum to learn about the island's history and cultural heritage. In the village of Sandy Ground, immerse yourself in the lively music scene and dance the night away to the sounds of reggae, soca, and calypso.

Nature enthusiasts will find plenty to explore in Anguilla. The island is home to two protected areas: the East End Pond and the Little Bay Marine Park. Take a guided tour to discover the diverse bird species that inhabit the wetlands of East End Pond or go snorkeling in the clear waters of the Marine Park to encounter vibrant coral reefs and a myriad of tropical fish.

For those seeking a touch of luxury and relaxation, Anguilla offers an impressive selection of upscale resorts, boutique hotels, and private villas. Many of these accommodations are situated along the stunning coastline, providing breathtaking views and direct access to the beach. From world-class spas to infinity pools overlooking the Caribbean Sea, these accommodations offer the perfect blend of comfort and serenity.

To get around the island, renting a car is a convenient option. Anguilla has well-maintained roads, and driving allows you to explore the island at your own pace. Alternatively, taxis are readily available, and some resorts offer shuttle services for their guests. Bicycles and scooters are also popular modes of transportation for shorter distances.

When planning your visit to Anguilla, keep in mind that the island enjoys a warm and tropical climate year-round. The peak tourist season typically falls between December and April when the weather is pleasant and dry. However, visiting during the shoulder seasons (May-June and November) can offer lower rates and fewer crowds while still enjoying favorable weather.

Anguilla's warm and welcoming locals contribute to the island's charm. Take the time to engage in conversations with the residents, who are known for their friendliness and hospitality. Embrace the island's laid-back lifestyle and let yourself unwind in the serene beauty of Anguilla.

As you explore Anguilla, remember to respect the environment and support sustainable tourism practices. The island is committed to preserving its natural beauty, so be mindful of your impact and follow any guidelines in place to protect the fragile ecosystems.

Antigua and Barbuda

Welcome to the stunning twin-island nation of Antigua and Barbuda! Located in the Caribbean Sea, this tropical paradise offers pristine beaches, crystal-clear waters, and a vibrant local culture. Whether you're seeking relaxation on the beach or thrilling adventures, Antigua and Barbuda have something for everyone. In this chapter, we will explore the islands in detail, including their history, culture, attractions, and activities, allowing you to get to know Antigua and Barbuda like a local.

Geography and Climate

Antigua and Barbuda consist of two main islands, Antigua and Barbuda, along with several smaller islands. Antigua, the largest of the two, is known for its 365 white sandy beaches, one for each day of the year. Barbuda, located to the north, offers a more secluded and untouched environment with its pink sand beaches and diverse wildlife.

The islands enjoy a tropical climate, characterized by warm temperatures and refreshing trade winds. The average temperature ranges from 77°F (25°C) in the winter months to 86°F (30°C) in the summer. The dry season, from December to April, is the most popular time to visit, offering clear skies and minimal rainfall.

History and Culture

Antigua and Barbuda have a rich history dating back thousands of years. The islands were inhabited by the indigenous Arawak and Carib peoples before being colonized by the Europeans. The British had a significant influence on the islands, which gained independence in 1981 but remains a member of the Commonwealth.

The culture of Antigua and Barbuda is a vibrant blend of African, European, and Caribbean traditions. The locals, known as Antiguans and Barbudans, are warm and welcoming, embracing their cultural heritage through music, dance, and cuisine. The islands are famous for their lively festivals, including the annual Carnival celebration, which showcases colorful costumes, calypso music, and spirited dancing.

Attractions and Activities

Beaches: Antigua boasts an abundance of breathtaking beaches. From the popular Dickenson Bay with its soft sands and clear waters to the tranquil Half Moon Bay known for its untouched beauty, there's a beach for every preference. You can indulge in various water activities such as snorkeling, paddleboarding, and kayaking.

Nelson's Dockyard: Located in English Harbour, Nelson's Dockyard is a UNESCO World Heritage Site and a must-visit attraction for history enthusiasts. This beautifully restored 18th-century naval base offers insight into Antigua's maritime past and provides stunning views of the harbor. Explore the museum, admire the historic buildings, and dine at one of the waterfront restaurants.

Shirley Heights: For panoramic views and a lively atmosphere, head to Shirley Heights. This hilltop lookout offers breathtaking vistas of English Harbor and is particularly popular during the Sunday evening sunset parties. Enjoy live music, savor local cuisine, and dance the night away to the rhythms of steel pan music.

Stingray City: Embark on a memorable adventure to Stingray City, located off the coast of Antigua. Here, you can swim and interact with friendly southern stingrays in their natural habitat. Guided tours provide a safe and educational experience, allowing you to learn about these fascinating creatures while enjoying a unique snorkeling or diving experience.

Barbuda's Frigate Bird Sanctuary: Take a day trip to Barbuda and visit the Frigate Bird Sanctuary. This protected area is home to the largest nesting colony of frigate birds in the Caribbean. Observe these magnificent birds in their natural habitat and marvel at their impressive wingspan during mating season.

Antigua Rainforest Canopy Tour: If you're seeking an adrenaline rush, embark on a thrilling zip line adventure through Antigua's lush rainforest. Soar through the treetops, experience breathtaking views, and learn about the local flora and fauna from knowledgeable guides.

Cuisine

Antigua and Barbuda offer a delectable culinary experience, blending traditional Caribbean flavors with international influences. Sample local dishes such as saltfish and fungi (a cornmeal-based dish), pepperpot (a hearty stew), and conch fritters. Don't miss out on the fresh seafood, including lobster, snapper, and mahi-mahi, caught daily by local fishermen. Pair your meal with a refreshing rum punch or a cold Wadadli beer, the local brew.

Getting Around

Antigua and Barbuda have a well-developed transportation infrastructure, making it easy to explore the islands. Taxis are readily available at the airport and major tourist areas, and drivers can provide island tours upon request. Rental cars are also popular, allowing you the freedom to explore at your own pace.

Saba

Welcome to the picturesque island of Saba, often referred to as the "Unspoiled Queen" of the Caribbean. Tucked away in the northeastern Caribbean Sea, this small but enchanting island is known for its dramatic landscapes, rich biodiversity, and a unique charm that captivates visitors. In this chapter, we will delve into the wonders of Saba, exploring its geography, culture, attractions, and activities, allowing you to discover the essence of this hidden gem like a local.

Geography and Climate

Saba is the smallest special municipality of the Netherlands, located just southwest of St. Maarten. Despite its small size, it boasts impressive topography, with Mount Scenery, an extinct volcano, rising to a height of 2,877 feet (877 meters), making it the highest point in the Kingdom of the Netherlands. Saba is also renowned for its rugged coastline, adorned with towering cliffs and secluded coves.

The island's tropical climate is characterized by consistent trade winds, offering a refreshing breeze throughout the year. The average temperature ranges from 77°F (25°C) to 86°F (30°C), providing pleasant conditions for outdoor activities. The rainy season, from May to November, brings occasional showers and lush greenery to the island.

History and Culture

Saba has a fascinating history shaped by the influences of different cultures. It was first inhabited by the Arawak and Carib peoples before being colonized by the Dutch in the 17th century. The island has maintained its ties to the Netherlands and is now an official part of the Dutch Caribbean.

The local culture of Saba is a fusion of Dutch, African, and Carib influences. The Saban people, known for their warmth and friendliness, take pride in their unique traditions and heritage. The island is home to skilled craftsmen who create intricate lacework, woodworking, and hand-painted souvenirs, reflecting the island's rich artistic heritage.

Attractions and Activities

Mount Scenery Hike: Embark on a memorable adventure by hiking to the summit of Mount Scenery. The trail winds through lush rainforest, showcasing Saba's diverse flora and fauna. At the peak, you'll be rewarded with breathtaking panoramic views of the surrounding islands and the Caribbean Sea.

Saba Marine Park: Dive into the crystal-clear waters of the Saba Marine Park, a protected marine reserve that encircles the entire island. Explore the vibrant coral reefs teeming with tropical fish, sea turtles, and other marine life. Snorkel or scuba dive in awe-inspiring sites such as Diamond Rock and Third Encounter, known for their underwater beauty.

The Bottom: Visit the charming capital of Saba, The Bottom. This quaint village is nestled at the foot of Mount Scenery and is characterized by colorful cottages and narrow streets. Explore the local shops, art galleries, and museums, and immerse yourself in the island's unique atmosphere.

Windwardside: Discover the picturesque village of Windwardside, known for its traditional Saban architecture and stunning views. Take a leisurely stroll along the streets lined with red-roofed cottages, explore the local boutiques, and indulge in delicious Caribbean cuisine at one of the charming restaurants.

Saba Heritage Center: Immerse yourself in the island's history at the Saba Heritage Center. This museum showcases artifacts, photographs, and exhibits that tell the story of Saba's past. Learn about the island's geological formation, the history of the indigenous people, and the influences of Dutch colonization.

Saba's Trail System: Lace up your hiking boots and explore Saba's extensive trail system, which crisscrosses the island. From gentle walks to challenging hikes, these well-maintained trails lead you through breathtaking scenery, including tropical forests, rocky cliffs, and hidden beaches. Don't miss the famous Sandy Cruz Trail, which offers magnificent views of the coastline.

Saba Carnival: Experience the vibrant energy of Saba during Carnival season, which takes place in late July and early August. Join in the colorful parades, lively music, and traditional dances as the island comes alive with festivities. It's an excellent opportunity to embrace the local culture and celebrate alongside the Saban community.

Cuisine

Saban cuisine is a delightful fusion of Caribbean and European flavors. Indulge in local dishes such as lobster, conch, and mahi-mahi, freshly caught by the island's fishermen. Sample traditional favorites like goat stew, rice and beans, and Johnny cakes, a type of savory bread. Don't forget to try Saba's famous banana bread, made with locally grown bananas and enjoyed as a delicious treat.

Getting Around

Saba's small size and rugged terrain make it best explored on foot or by taxi. The island's main road, aptly named "The Road," winds its way through the villages, offering stunning views along the way. Taxis are readily available at the airport and can take you to your desired destination. It's worth noting that Saba does not have a rental car service, ensuring a peaceful and tranquil atmosphere.

Conclusion

As the sun dipped below the horizon, painting the sky in hues of orange and pink, I couldn't help but reflect on the incredible journey I had just experienced in St. Kitts and Nevis. From the moment I stepped off the plane, I knew that this Caribbean paradise would steal my heart and leave me with cherished memories for a lifetime.

My vacation in St. Kitts and Nevis was a perfect blend of relaxation, adventure, and cultural immersion. The stunning beaches, fringed with palm trees and lapped by turquoise waters, provided the perfect backdrop for lazy days of sunbathing and beachcombing. Each morning, I woke up to the sound of waves crashing on the shore, knowing that another day of paradise awaited.

The friendly locals welcomed me with open arms, sharing their rich history and vibrant culture. From exploring the historic Brimstone Hill Fortress, a UNESCO World Heritage Site, to wandering the charming streets of

Basseterre, the capital city, I felt a deep connection to the island's past and its people.

The verdant rainforests of St. Kitts offered thrilling adventures for the nature enthusiast in me. Hiking through the lush trails, I discovered hidden waterfalls, exotic flora, and encountered playful monkeys swinging through the trees. A visit to the Wingfield Estate, a former sugar plantation, gave me insight into the island's colonial past and its transition to a thriving agricultural hub.

Snorkeling and scuba diving in the crystal-clear waters of St. Kitts and Nevis were an absolute highlight. The vibrant coral reefs teemed with colorful marine life, and swimming alongside sea turtles was a dream come true. I also had the opportunity to explore shipwrecks and underwater caves, adding an element of mystery to my underwater escapades.

One of the most memorable experiences was the authentic Kittitian and Nevisian cuisine. From fresh seafood caught that very day to mouthwatering jerk chicken and savory goat stew, every dish was a delightful explosion of flavors.

I indulged in local delicacies and sipped on fruity rum cocktails while watching the sunsets over the horizon—a perfect way to end each day.

As the days turned into nights, I found myself engulfed in the pulsating rhythm of the local music and dance. Calypso and soca tunes filled the air, and I couldn't resist moving my feet to the infectious beat. The warm and hospitable locals encouraged me to join in the festivities, and I danced the night away with newfound friends.

As my vacation in St. Kitts and Nevis came to an end, I realized that this enchanting destination had left an indelible mark on my soul. The breathtaking landscapes, the vibrant culture, and the genuine warmth of the people had touched me in a profound way.

As I boarded the plane to return home, I knew that a piece of St. Kitts and Nevis would forever remain with me. The memories of lazy days on the beach, thrilling adventures in the rainforest, and the laughter-filled evenings with locals would be cherished forever.

St. Kitts and Nevis had given me more than just a vacation—it had given me an experience of a lifetime. It had rekindled my love for nature, opened my heart to new cultures, and reminded me of the beauty of simple joys. I left with a promise to return one day, to relive the magic of this Caribbean gem once again. Until then, the memories of my unforgettable journey in St. Kitts and Nevis would sustain me, like a gentle sea breeze, reminding me of the paradise I had experienced.